whales to see The

whaLes to see The

GLENDON and KATHRYN

SWARTHOUT

———

Illustrations by Paul Bacon

DOUBLEDAY & COMPANY, INC.

GARDEN CITY, NEW YORK

Library of Congress Cataloging in Publication Data
Swarthout, Glendon Fred
Whales to see the
SUMMARY: A group of children with learning
disabilities have problems coping with the many
social pressures they face everyday.
[1. Learning disabilities—Fiction. 2. Prejudices—Fiction]
I. Swarthout, Kathryn, joint author. II. Title.
PZ7.S9727We   [Fic]
ISBN 0-385-09873-1 Trade
0-385-09874-X Prebound
Library of Congress Catalog Card Number 74-33692

whales to see The

They that go down to the sea in ships,
that do business in great waters;
these see the works of the Lord,
and His wonders in the deep.

Psalms 107:23–24

one

Dee-Dee was wakened by the clock radio beside her bed. She lazed for a time, listening to Id and the Egos do their smash hard-rock single "Wherever You Go, There You Are!" and hoping the DJ would spin a ballad by Gary Garloo next. He didn't, of course. He went into a commercial about foot powder while she let her eyes drift the familiar room—white and gold dresser and desk, portable color TV, white wallpaper with pink angels, gold drapes which fell from ceiling to carpet in rich folds, California sunshine surfing through the window. Over the commercial she heard the whine of her father's electric razor and the clink of dishes in the kitchen downstairs, which would be her mother getting breakfast, probably eggs, ick.

She stared at the telephone on the table beside her. I need a telephone about as much as I need foot powder, she admitted. I never call anybody and nobody ever calls me. If I went to a regular school instead of a special school I'd probably talk half the night every night with girlfriends because I'd have girlfriends, maybe even boyfriends. Maybe even Mr. Wonderful would give me a buzz sometime.

Yikes! She burst out of the bedclothes and punched the radio off so hard that it slammed into the wall. This was the day before tomorrow and tomorrow was the day!

And we'll make it, she told herself, we'll make it through today okay. I am very optimistic. Miss Fish will keep the room under control and the kids will pop their pills and be super-cool and ultra-good and nobody will dare try to call it off.

Dee-Dee made her hands into fists. Nobody better try, she warned the world. If we're cheated out of tomorrow I'll sneak out tonight and set fire to it and burn the whole school to the ground, I swear I will.

John woke when he hit the floor. He shared the bed with his two little brothers, and every night they had bad dreams and yelled and kicked him out on the floor. This was the third time tonight, but it was already daylight and time to get up anyway.

He climbed into a pair of pants and put on his glasses and tiptoed through the house and outdoors to the neighbors' front yard. Their morning paper had already been delivered, so he picked it up and had his usual survey of the television program page to see what would be on the tube that night. His mother claimed she couldn't afford a daily paper, and once, when he suggested she could if she would cut down on the wine, she had hit him such a crack that he heard sweet music without a radio. He studied every channel listing.

The only good program he could find was a *National Geographic* special about a lost tribe in the jungles of Africa, and since he didn't know any lost tribes and hadn't traveled to Africa lately he decided to give it a look.

Refolding the paper neatly, he returned to his house wondering what to get himself for breakfast. Cold cereal was out because the milk, he knew, was sour. Toast would be okay if the toaster worked, which it didn't. If there was ham he'd have ham and eggs if there were eggs, but there was neither. Then he remembered a can of sardines in the cupboard.

He crept into the kitchen, found the can, opened it, and began to eat and at the same time, to get the sardines down successfully, imagined what his ideal breakfast would be. It would be a double banana split with whipped cream and marshmallow and crushed nuts and cherries.

One last, limp sardine to go. John stared at it, and that made him think of Miss Fish, and she reminded him that this was the day before tomorrow and tomorrow was the day of what she called their "grand and glorious adventure." Well maybe, thought John, and maybe not. Most likely not. Because we'll never make it through today. Somebody will do something and the whole room will go into orbit and Miss Fish will push the panic button and Mr. Driggs the old grouch will say, That does it, sorry, tomorrow is off, you can't go.

He took the sardine by the tail, held it high, tilted his head back, opened his mouth wide, closed his eyes hard, thought—look out teeth, look out gums, look out guts, here it comes!—let it drop, swallowed, opened his eyes, and made a horrible face. So long, sardine. Farewell, grand and glorious adventure.

It was no different, Dee-Dee would sometimes stick her chin out and say, from an ordinary sixth-grade schoolroom. It had desks and chairs and blackboards and shelves of books and a record player and pictures on the walls and wide windows. It had a teacher at a desk. Miss Fish was a prim and proper spinster of sixty-two who possessed, in spite of her age, a spry heart.

Ordinary ha, John would say. The room was really weird if you looked closely at it. For one thing, there were only ten kids in the class, six boys and four girls. The boys' names were Ralph and John and Arnold and Myron and Mike and Pablito. The girls were Sandra and Anne and Dee-Dee and Musette. For another, there were two "offices" in the room, as there were in every classroom in the school. The "offices" were three-sided wooden boxes, their high sides covered with vinyl, and once a boy or girl was seated within at a small desk, he couldn't see out nor could anyone outside see in. It was no disgrace to be asked to go into an office for a while, and the teachers found them very useful. And what about the ten pill bottles lined up on a shelf? Miss Fish gave the children one pill early in the morning and a second after lunch—a tranquilizer or a suppressant or a stimulant, depending on what the doctor had prescribed in each case—so that they could cope with their problems and pay complete attention to their work. And hey, John would say, what about the panic button? You

14

might not see it, but it was there, hidden under the edge of Miss Fish's desk. Each teacher had one. When she pushed it, bells rang in the office of Mr. Driggs, the principal, and in the rooms of the other teachers so that they could hurry to her assistance.

But if you had stepped into their sixth-grade room during the last hour of school this particular afternoon, you couldn't have cared less whether it was ordinary or weird or who was right, Dee-Dee or John. In a second you'd have known in your bones that something was about to happen. The walls seemed to crawl, the floor to giggle hysterically, the air itself to itch with electricity. It was as though the ten boys and girls had waited too long for something, had held their excitement and anticipation too tightly—as though the room was loaded and ready and waiting to explode.

Miss Fish left her desk. To keep the class busy for the last hour she had put them to work painting watercolor pictures of the experience they were to have tomorrow. Now she peeked over their shoulders to see what they were painting. She had just peeked over John's when Mike stood up and poured his watercolors over Dee-Dee's dress.

"Ohhhhhh!" cried Dee-Dee.

"She! Pinched! Me!" cried Mike.

"I did not!" cried Dee-Dee. "I'll kill him!"

"But if you did that," said Miss Fish, who was already mopping Dee-Dee's dress with Kleenex, "poor Mike couldn't go with us tomorrow, could he? And then wouldn't we all be miserable?"

"I've! Got! To! Go! Tomorrow!" cried Mike, who had much difficulty getting words out.

"Of course you have," said Miss Fish. "Mike, dear, do you mind going into an office for a while? Take your picture and brush and I'll bring you more colors. And you, Dee-Dee, go on with yours—it's lovely, dear."

Dee-Dee sat down and Miss Fish brought new colors to Mike, then had to bring the other things. Mike could seldom remember more than one instruction out of three. In this case he had gone into an office but forgotten his brush and picture. Miss Fish praised his picture, then began again her patrol of the room.

John could feel her peeking over his shoulder. He didn't mind because he considered his picture terrific, or at least great. He had the sea just right, dark blue and smooth, and the sky, light blue and bright. And he had everything in its proper place. The lower section of the boat, or hull, was entirely under water, while the upper section, cabin and bridge and mast, was separated from the hull and floated on the surface. And way up in the sky was a whale. And on top of the whale's back, with smoke curling out, was the funnel of the boat. And painted in the sky was the picture's title: "WHALES TO SEE THE."

He waited for her praise. "John, dear," she said finally, "that's very good. The colors are true and the boat looks very real. There's just one small thing, though. Your title. You have the word 'WHALES' at the beginning. Don't you mean to call it 'TO SEE THE WHALES'?"

John scowled at his title. As soon as she said it, he knew she was right, but who cared about a title? It burned him up that she should nit-pick a work of art as terrific or at least as great as this one. So he scowled up at her, then put down his brush, folded his hands on the desk, and stared straight ahead. He sat without moving. He could sit that way all day. John was small for his age. He wore thick glasses, and at the tip of each bow, behind his ear, was a tiny battery-powered hearing aid. Whenever he wanted, he could shut out sound by turning off his hearing aids. And whenever he wanted, as he did now, he could shut out everybody and everything by turning himself off.

Just then Musette hit Ralph over the head with a book.

Miss Fish put Musette in the other office, and after noticing the black girl had her left shoe on her right foot, had her exchange them. She contented Ralph by praising his picture. Then she went to her desk again to take stock and check the clock. She had Musette in one office, Mike in the other, and John had isolated himself in his own.

They'd never make it. She could sense the tension rising in the room. But she couldn't give them extra drugs. No, if the ten of them went off like a bomb, she'd have to rely on the panic button.

Oh Lord, prayed Sarah Fish silently, I'm in a ticklish situation here. If I have to push that button in the next twenty-three minutes, we may not be allowed to go tomorrow. You see, Mr. Driggs, our principal, has been against it from the beginning, and so have some of the staff and some of my parents, too. They think the children won't be able to handle the freedom, that they'll burst like balloons and I'll lose control and terrible things may happen. Stuff-and-nonsense. You and I know better. We know that I'm the very special teacher of a very special class in a very special school—and with Your help I can manage them. Besides, as I've told Mr. Driggs and the staff and the parents, these boys and girls simply must have this grand and glorious adventure. Thanks to their problems, most of them have never been anywhere or done anything. This is a chance for them to get out into the world and see with their own eyes Your wonders. They mustn't be denied that chance. But if I have to push the button now, Mr. Driggs may say, Sarah, I told you so, I forbid you to take them tomorrow. So please, please, Lord, keep my children calm and patient and let us get through the next twenty-two minutes so that tomorrow we can—oh no, dammit, no!

Mike had just jumped up and tipped over his office.

The room exploded.
Miss Fish started for Mike.
Anne reached over, seized Sandra's picture, and tore it in half.
Miss Fish turned toward Anne.
Arnold left his desk and began to run round and round the room as though he were in a race.
Miss Fish tried to catch him.
Pablito, a brown-eyed Mexican-American boy, hit My-

ron. Myron hit Pablito. A fistfight began.

Miss Fish attempted to separate them.

Dee-Dee leaped up to attack Mike and, stumbling into Musette's office, tipped it over with a crash.

Trying to pull Myron and Pablito apart, Miss Fish got an elbow in the stomach that knocked the wind out of her.

Sandra began to cry.

Gasping for breath, Miss Fish moved to console her.

Musette pulled books from the shelves and threw them at Ralph.

Miss Fish ran to stop her.

Dee-Dee screamed at the top of her voice.

Miss Fish clapped a hand over Dee-Dee's mouth. Dee-Dee bit her.

John scurried from his desk into a corner of the room and buried his face in a curtain.

Miss Fish went to talk to him and was run into by Arnold the racer. She fell backward and stuck her foot into a wastebasket.

Angered by what Arnold had done to her, Mike caught him and wrestled him to the floor.

Deafened, her hand hurting, and out of breath, Miss Fish pulled her foot from the wastebasket. Anne and Sandra were bawling at each other and Mike and Arnold were wrestling on the floor and Dee-Dee was screaming and Musette was throwing books at Ralph and John was hiding in a curtain and Myron and Pablito were fistfighting. She headed for her desk, reaching for the edge and the panic button. Just as she found it she had the idea.

Hopping over Mike and Arnold, she snatched a record up and put it on the turntable. Snapping the machine on, she turned the volume up full.

Suddenly the room boomed with sounds. They were astounding sounds. Once heard, they could never be forgotten. You heard them when you were busy in the day and there were people about and the sun was shining. You heard them in the night, when you awoke and the house was still and you were lonely. They were sounds which, until only recently, no human ear had known.

They made magic in the room. Anne and Sandra ceased to cry. Mike and Arnold let go of each other and got to their feet. Dee-Dee stopped screaming. Musette threw no more books at Ralph. John dropped the curtain and uncovered his face. Myron and Pablito lowered their fists.

Miss Fish returned to her desk. The ten boys and girls returned to their desks. Everyone listened.

What they listened to was a record called *Songs of the Humpbacked Whale*. Miss Fish had bought it for her room a month ago, when they had first begun to plan their trip. She had played it for them almost every day since then, but today it had slipped her mind. She had heard the record herself on television. Scientists had determined to find out if whales communicated with each other. Putting to sea in a research vessel, and locating several pods of the huge mammals, they dragged behind the stern, below the surface and among the whales, a recording device. And what the device picked up, the scientists had transcribed onto a record.

Whales did indeed communicate with one another under water, and over great distances, since sound travels more swiftly through water than it does through air. The whales called to each other. To some, the sounds they made were like the bellowing of mighty ships in harbor. To others, the sounds were like those of great gold and silver horns, blown long and loud and echoing from mountain peak to mountain peak. Some said the sounds were sad, others said they were full of joy and life unbounded. To everyone, however, they were new and rare and beautiful.

The buzzer buzzed. School was over.

Miss Fish stepped to the player and shut it off. "Well," she said, "we made it. Bully for us. You may go now, but remember. Eight-thirty in the morning. And do bring sack lunches. I'll meet you out in front, by the bus. Now everyone go to bed early and get a good night's sleep, and when you open your eyes in the morning—wow!"

She smiled at them. But to her surprise, no one moved. They sat at their desks like bumps on a log. "What's wrong?" she asked. "School's out—you can go. What's wrong?"

Anne opened her mouth. So did Myron, and Arnold, and Musette.

"Well?" asked Miss Fish.

"Before we go—" Anne began.

"Could we—" interrupted Myron.

"Can we hear—" interrupted Arnold.

"The rest of the record?" interrupted Musette.

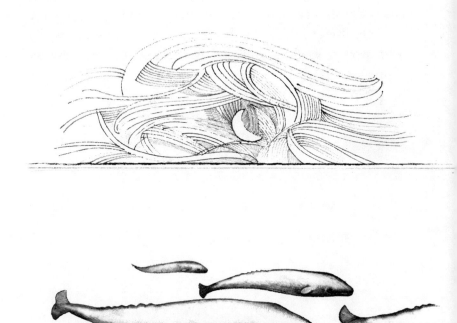

Miss Fish smiled. Inside her spry heart, a little silver horn was blown. "Of course you can," she said. "The bus can wait."

She turned the record over and started the machine and stood where she was, looking into one child's face and then another, into the blue and brown and black eyes wide with mystery, shining with anticipation. And then Sarah Fish closed her own eyes and listened with her children to the songs from under the sea, songs without words, songs as old as the oceans and as new as hope.

two

"Your dress," sighed her mother, "your poor dress. What did you do this time?"

"Me? Why does it always have to be me?"

"It usually is."

"Well, this time it wasn't," said Dee-Dee. "Mike poured his watercolors all over me. So there."

"And then what happened?"

"Nothing right away. But in a little while—wow—we went crazy, the whole room. The boys were fighting and Arnold was running around and around and Anne and Sandra were crying and John was hiding in a curtain and Musette was throwing books and I was, was—"

"Was what?"

"Nothing."

"Dee-Dee."

"Okay, I was screaming."

"Why?"

"I don't know. Everybody was going crazy."

"Of course."

"Of course?"

"This ridiculous trip tomorrow."

Dee-Dee stood in the living room of her home in the Point Loma section of San Diego. The house was large and made of brick, with green lawns and cypress trees, and it was only two blocks from the ocean. She stood facing her mother, her arms full of books.

"I've been opposed to it from the beginning," her mother continued, "and so have some of the other parents. We've told Mr. Driggs as much. And what happened this afternoon is proof we were right. Miss Fish has you all higher than kites over a stupid field trip—and if she can't control ten children in her own room, what will she do on a boat? Sarah Fish may be a good teacher, but she's also a sentimental old idiot."

"You shut up about her!"

Angrily, Dee-Dee dropped her books on an endtable. They thudded down, not where she expected but inches away, hitting a crystal ashtray and sending it flying off the table onto the tile floor, where it shattered into a jillion pieces. Dee-Dee stared at the floor, unable to meet her mother's eyes.

"That was your father's favorite ashtray," said her mother. "And very expensive."

"I'm sorry."

"Please go up and take a nap now."

"I'm not sleepy."

"You may not be sleepy, but you're wound as tight as a guitar string—thanks to Miss Fish."

"Can I ride my bike afterward?"

"Certainly. If you use training wheels."

Dee-Dee stamped her foot. "Training wheels! And

have every kid on the block laugh at me?"

Her mother sighed. "Which is better, dear? To be laughed at or to hit a bush or a tree and fall off and hurt yourself and have the children yell 'Re-tard! Re-tard!' at you?"

Dee-Dee frowned. "I won't ride at all. Can I go swimming?"

"If you take a nap."

"Oh, all right." Dee-Dee turned, went to the door, thought of something, turned again. "I know why you really don't want me to go tomorrow."

"Why?"

"You think I'll do something bad, and you'll be ashamed of me. Well, I won't. I'm perfectly all right."

"Of course," said her mother, glancing at the shattered glass on the floor.

Dee-Dee stamped up the stairs, stumbling only once, and into her room, where she slammed the door and threw herself on the bed. Clicking on her transistor radio, she hid it under her pillow and lay for half an hour watching the clock beside her bed. She was too nervous to nap. Eight-thirty tomorrow morning was only sixteen hours or so away now. She twisted. She turned. She tried to lose herself listening to the Garbagemen, to the Peanut Butter Band, to Hub Kapp and the Wheels, to the DJ's platter-patter, but she couldn't. She wished she had a sister to talk to, or even a grungy brother. An only child is lonely, she thought, but I'm not a child any more. I'm twelve years old going on thirteen. And apraxic and hyperkinetic, too.

Dee-Dee's mother and father knew that something was wrong with her as soon as she began to walk. She stumbled. She dropped and bumped into and tripped over things. They took her to doctors, who told them she was "neurologically impaired." And what did that mean? they asked. It meant, the doctors said, that as a result of a minor accident at birth, or to some error of nature in her bodily chemistry, her central nervous system did not work properly. The doctors didn't know exactly what the cause was, but in Dee-Dee's case she was a victim of "apraxia," or "impaired motor control." This meant that she did not have normal control of her arms and legs, and so her movements. She was like an automobile in motion, sometimes, without a driver. And when would their little girl recover from this handicap? her parents asked the doctors. Probably never, was the answer.

Her father carried Dee-Dee from the doctors' offices to the family car in his arms. He was a lawyer, a grown man, but he was crying. So was her mother.

But her troubles truly began when she went to school. She couldn't play games at recess because she couldn't throw or catch a ball or run very fast. The other children called her "clumsy" at first, then "Re-tard! Re-tard!" She hit them, she bit them. When her teacher interfered, she hit and bit her. She was often in tears, and equally as often in the principal's office. And she learned slowly. She had to take the first grade over, and when her parents were told she must repeat the second grade as well, they made more appointments with more doctors.

This time the doctors said Dee-Dee was a victim of "hyperkinesia." And what did that mean? asked her parents. It meant that due to the same mysterious causes as apraxia, her other handicap, she was subject to "minimal brain dysfunction." And that meant she would have learning problems. And reacting to these problems, she might be overactive and aggressive toward other children. If she were sometimes like an automobile without a driver, sometimes the engine of the automobile wouldn't run smoothly either. What could be done for their little girl? her parents asked. Certain drugs might help, was the answer, and these would be prescribed, but the best thing for Dee-Dee would be to place her in a special school, where special teachers could help her personally to learn and grow and one day return to regular school and one day, still later, to live a happy, useful life.

This time, when they left the doctors' offices to go to the family car, Dee-Dee tripping over a bump in the sidewalk, her father and mother couldn't even see her fall through their tears.

When her half hour was over, she jumped up, put on her suit, and went downstairs, through the house, and outdoors to the swimming pool. Her mother followed her and sat down on a bench by the pool while Dee-Dee walked into the pool and struck out for the deep end.

She swam like no one else. She couldn't seem to use her arms and legs in the same rhythm, so she thrashed and splashed wildly, sending spray in all directions, hauling herself by sheer determination swiftly through the water, tiring after two or three noisy laps up and down the pool. Then she rested at the side, holding herself with elbows over the coping.

"Why d'you always watch me?" she asked her mother. "Because I swim funny?"

"I like to."

"Ha. You probably think I'll drown."

"No, but you do have physical problems, Dee-Dee, and I like to keep an eye on you."

Dee-Dee changed the subject. "Now only about fifteen hours."

"Fifteen hours? Till what?"

"Till we go tomorrow morning."

"Oh. Well, we'll talk about that tonight, your father and I, and decide."

"Decide?"

"Whether or not we think it advisable for you to go."

Dee-Dee's chin dropped. Then, as disbelief gave way to anger, she clenched her fists. "You mean you might not let me go? This late?" she cried. "You wouldn't dare—you wouldn't!"

Her mother frowned. "Dee-Dee, dear, I'm sorry. You may not believe it sometimes, but we love you terribly. Maybe because you have problems, you're even more precious to us than normal children are to their parents. And since you are, we have a special responsibility to do what we think best for you, no matter how much it may hurt." Her mother rose. "Now I won't discuss it further. We'll decide tonight."

30

Dee-Dee let go of the coping and began to slap the water with both hands as though she were slapping her mother. "You wouldn't dare!" she screamed. "You wouldn't, wouldn't dare!"

The three of them got through the evening meal very well, although Dee-Dee spilled a glass of milk. Her father talked about things at the office. Dee-Dee described again how Miss Fish almost had to push the panic button that afternoon. Her mother was silent. Then, while she was having pudding for dessert, Dee-Dee dropped a spoon with a clang.

"I can't help it," she said defiantly. "I just have to know."

"I told her you and I would discuss it and decide tonight," her mother explained to her father. "Whether or not we think it wise for her to go tomorrow. We can call Miss Fish tonight if necessary."

"Oh? Oh well, that makes sense," said her father. "Doesn't it to you, Duck?" he asked his daughter. He called her "Duck" because he said she took to water as naturally as one.

"I never wanted to do anything so much in my whole life," she said, sticking the spoon into her pudding like a dagger. "You're cruel to make me wait."

Her father looked at her wearily. "You don't mean that, Duck. We make mistakes, I'm sure, but we try to do what's best. We buy you a bike with training wheels. We build a pool because swimming's the best exercise for you. We pay two hundred dollars a month to send you to a special school, and—"

"Money," Dee-Dee sniffed. "If that's what you care about, all tomorrow'll cost you is a sack lunch."

It was quiet at the table.

"That was cruel of you, Dee-Dee," said her mother.

Dee-Dee knew it was, but she would not apologize.

"I suppose the reason we can hurt each other so easily," said her father, "is because we love each other so much." He looked at his daughter. "So very, very much."

She couldn't meet his eyes. Tears welled up in her own. "Love ha," she said stubbornly.

It was quiet again.

"Please go to your room, dear," said her mother. "Your father and I will let you know about tomorrow in a few minutes."

Dee-Dee sprang from her chair. "You don't love me— you hate me! You're ashamed of me! You wish you hadn't borne me!"

And running from the room, she stumbled up the stairs to her bedroom, slammed the door, and would have thrown herself on her bed except that suddenly she remembered what was in her dresser drawer. The remembering frightened her. Because this might be the time.

Instead of lying down and beating the bed and crying her eyes out, she turned on a lamp and began to do other things. First she opened a window. The night air was damp with fog, seeping in from the Pacific. Then she gazed at the poster-picture of Gary Garloo, the terrific-teen-age-outfar-superstar-singer-and-softrock-swinger she had tacked up on a wall. He was so darling and dreamy she could die. Then she locked her bedroom door, opened the lower dresser drawer and, sitting on the floor, searched under socks and undies till she found them. She brought them out handful by handful, heaping them on the carpet before her.

There must have been a hundred matchfolders. She'd been picking them up everywhere for the last year, and hiding them for the time, the perfect time. And since she hadn't had to use them to burn down her school, this might be it. She knew exactly what she'd do. If her mother and father said no, she couldn't go, she'd wait till they were in bed and asleep. Then she'd put the pile of matches under one of the drapes and use one match to light it. The whole heap would blaze up— the drapes would catch fire—in seconds the room would be a furnace—then the whole house would go up in flames and burn to the ground and in the last moment of smoke and pain before she died she'd be glad because she'd never fall or smash or stumble or trip or be clumsy again and in the last moment of smoke and pain before they died her father and mother would be sorry they'd said no.

A knock at her door.

Dee-Dee stood up, a matchfolder in her hand. "What is it?"

"Dee-Dee, dear, we've decided." It was her mother's voice. "We think you should go tomorrow, after all, and have an absolutely marvelous time."

Dee-Dee dropped the matches. She wanted to cry buckets and say, Oh, wow, you don't know it but I was about to destroy us all even though I know you love me

33

and were deciding for my own good, but oh, wow, am I glad I didn't, because I love you, too!

"You can even bring a whale home for a pet," added her father. "We'll keep it in the pool and feed it pudding and teach it to ride a bike."

Dee-Dee wanted to giggle. But I can't giggle or tell them what I almost did either, she thought. That's what a child would do, and I'm twelve going on thirteen, so I'm not a child. I may be apraxic and hyperkinetic, but I'm definitely not a child.

"Thank you very much, Father and Mother," she said instead, keeping her voice calm and adult. "Thank you very much."

John hopped off the special school bus. Rather than scuffing along the dusty street to his house, he cut between houses and sneaked through the eucalyptus trees along the edge of the ravine, keeping out of sight of the other kids in the neighborhood. They were already home from school, and already outdoors playing, and if he passed by they'd shout "Re-tard! Re-tard!" If he turned off his hearing aids, that would make them mad. Some lunk of a boy would hit him and he'd have to fight back and go home with a bloody nose or a loose tooth.

He came up behind his house, which was a "leaner." It leaned toward the east, since the wind usually blew from the west, from the ocean. John was sure that if the wind ever blew from the east, the house would fall down. It was inland of the ocean in San Diego, not far in miles from where Dee-Dee lived but far in every other way. John's mother was on welfare, he had two sisters and two brothers, and the house was rented.

One of his fathers had put an old car up on cement blocks in the back yard, intending to repair and get it running one day. John couldn't remember whether that one was his real father or not, but the man had gone away and never been seen again and left the car without doing a thing to it. John's brothers and sisters and the neighbor kids had done a great deal. The windows were broken, the seats and floor mats and wires and parts were taken out, everything else was dusty and rusty. John had got the best things, though.

Pitching his books through a broken window of the car, he lurked along the edge of the ravine to some bushes and, ducking in, rolled out his prize possessions. What he'd salvaged from the old car was two tires. They were beautiful. They'd kept their round, the tread was good, and he washed them often to keep a bright black sheen.

He rolled them to the rim of the ravine. The land fell away abruptly below him, and a well-worn path led to the bottom.

He stood motionless for a moment, a tire on each side of him, a hand gripping the tread of each. His heart began to pound. He took a deep breath and summoned up his strength. Then, when he could wait no longer, he gave the tires a mighty shove.

Over the rim they went! Down the steep side of the ravine they rolled, faster and faster! Sixty, seventy, eighty, ninety feet downward they sped while he watched, hypnotized and thrilled! To the bottom, across

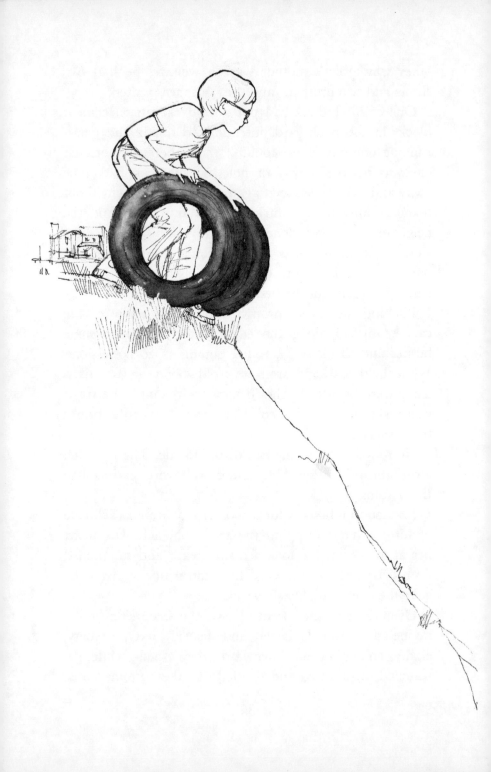

the bottom, up the other side in a blur they rolled—ten, fifteen, twenty feet upward, by themselves!

When they wobbled, stopped, tipped over, John let go his breath, took another, and started down the path himself. Crossing the bottom, he climbed to the two tires, bent down, put an arm through each, hoisted them onto his shoulders, turned and walked down, across the bottom, and panting with the effort, the tires growing heavier and heavier on his slight shoulders, trudged up the ninety feet to the place at the rim of the ravine where he had started. He let the tires slide down his arms to an upright position on the ground, turned himself between them so that he was looking into the deep ravine again, got a good grip on each tread, and stood motionless, resting.

His heart slowed. But soon it began to pound again. He took a deep breath and summoned up his strength. Then, when he could wait no longer, he gave the tires a mighty shove. Over the rim they went!

It was not John's mother who discovered that something was wrong with him, but his second-grade teacher. He had repeated the first grade because he had so much trouble learning to read. Toward the end of the second grade, when his mother was told he would have to repeat that grade as well, the teacher advised her to have John examined by a doctor. This she did, at the county hospital, after hours of waiting. The doctor asked her if she recalled having German measles while she was carrying John. Yes, she did recall. Ah, the doctor said, he thought as much. The fact was that John was a "rubella baby." Her illness had impaired his hearing. He needed hearing aids, which she should get at once. And not only that, John had a second handicap. He was dyslexic. "Dyslexia" was a condition of childhood the causes of which no one knew exactly. Dyslexic children sometimes saw letters in a word or words in a sentence out of order, and this made them slow readers. Sometimes, too, they couldn't put things together correctly. Parts of scenes were like pieces of a jigsaw puzzle they couldn't fit into the whole. Such children needed special attention, the doctor said, and John should be taken out of regular school and placed at once in a special school.

John's mother sat as though she hadn't heard. One of her girls tugged at her skirt. Another crawled across the floor. A boy bawled. Finally she said she couldn't afford either hearing aids or a special school. Her husband had deserted her, she was on welfare. The county would provide John with hearing aids, the doctor assured her, and the state of California would pay the two hundred dollars a month for special school. He would give her a letter, he said, which she must give to her social caseworker the next time the caseworker came by.

But it was almost Christmas before John's mother remembered she had put the letter away somewhere and forgotten where. By the time she found it, and gave it to the caseworker, John was failing second grade a second time. Matters moved quickly then, however. He had his hearing aids within two weeks, and a supply of spare batteries. Within another two weeks he was enrolled in a special school.

Down the steep side of the ravine the two tires rolled, faster and faster! Sixty, seventy, eighty, ninety feet downward they sped while John watched, hypnotized and thrilled! To the bottom, across the bottom, up the other side in a blur they rolled—ten, fifteen, twenty feet upward, by themselves!

When they wobbled, stopped, tipped over, John let go his breath, went down and brought the tires back over his shoulders to the rim of the ravine again, then rested. Soon his heart beat fast with anticipation, and he gave the tires a mighty shove. Over the rim they went!

John could roll his tires into the ravine and bring them up and roll them down again hour after hour every day after school and usually did. Other kids would wander along occasionally and ask to try it, and he'd let them, but they grew bored after a roll or two. They said it was a dumb game. Only a re-tard, they said, would find it fun.

John knew better. It depended on your imagination. If you had no imagination, of course it was a dumb game. But if you did, and used it, rolling tires into a ravine could be really exciting. Speeding down the steep side, the tires might be cars on a roller-coaster, or tanks rumbling to meet the enemy in a war, or runners in an Olympic dash for a gold medal, or racing cars roaring toward the finish line and fame and fortune. Or they might be just plain ordinary people, with warts and bowlegs and weak eyes and bad breath and fat, just plain ordinary people running side by side and proving how fast they could run if they truly wanted to. The important thing was—the tires did it on their own. After that first shove over the rim, no hand guided or helped them. They made their own speed, they took their own direction, and nothing could stop them. Nothing, that was, except the other side of the ravine. But the other important thing was—they attempted that, too. They rushed at the wall of the other side and tried, tried, tried to climb to the top. They never gave up, the way he often did. That they never made it didn't matter. They tried, they tried with all their rubber hearts to reach the top. And one day, John knew in his own heart, one wonderful day, all by themselves they would.

After supper he read a book on his bed in his bedroom, or rather the bed and the bedroom he shared with his younger brothers. Then he went out into the living room, which was also the dining room. His mother and brothers and sisters were watching wrestling on the small black-and-white TV.

"Hey," he said loudly, to make himself heard over the grunts and groans of the wrestlers and the cheers and jeers of the crowd. "Hey, can I watch something else for a while?"

"Something else what?" asked his mother. She was drinking wine from a glass, which she did most evenings watching TV. She kept four bottles of wine on a shelf over the kitchen sink and drank from different ones at different times. She called them her "boyfriends," and had named them "Bob," "Bernie," "Rafe," and "William." She was having a little "Rafe" tonight. "Something else what?" she repeated.

"It's a *National Geographic* special," John said. "About a lost tribe living in the jungles of Africa."

"Phooey," sneered his brothers.

"I like wrestling," said a sister.

"Me too," said the other. "Who wants to know about some dumb old tribe in some jungle?"

"I do," John said. "So should you, and the rest of you kids. It's a good thing to know about other people far away, how they live and stuff like that."

"What's good about it?" demanded a brother.

"Get outa my way!" a sister shrilled at him. "You're blocking my view! Ma, make 'im move!"

"Because that's how you learn about the world and about yourself," John said. "Don't you want to learn?"

"Crush 'im, squush 'im!" cried a brother as one wrestler jumped up and down on the other.

"Ma, make 'em shut up!" whined a sister. "I can't hear nothing!"

"Don't you?" John demanded.

"Don't I what?"

"Want to learn!"

"Learn what?"

John gave up and appealed to his mother. "Ma, they've watched wrestling for an hour. Could I please watch something I want for just a half hour?"

She smiled and nodded, and though John wasn't sure she understood, he went to the TV and switched channels till he found his show. Immediately his brothers and sisters set up a howl.

"Ma! Wah! Ma! Wah!"

John paid no attention, but sat down where he could see. In the center of their village in the jungles of Africa, the lost tribe was doing a wild dance, leaping about and shaking spears. His brothers and sisters took one look and started to do their own dance, leaping about and shaking their arms and being so noisy that John couldn't hear the sound from the set—yells of the warriors and pounding of the drums.

"Ma, I can't hear!" he shouted.

She smiled and nodded. She never seemed to mind what was on the set so long as the set was on.

He turned it off. "Ma, they're making so much noise I can't hear—it isn't fair."

She scowled at her other four. "Now you be still or I'll whup you."

They made faces at John and were quiet while he turned the TV on again and sat down to watch. But they were really mad at him now, and they knew their mother's threats were empty ones, so after a minute or two they started to torment the older brother who had cheated them out of their wrestling.

"Whatcha see, John?" asked a sister.

"Everything upside down?" asked the other.

"Where's the monkeys? On the ground?" asked a brother.

"An' where's the people? In the trees?" asked the other.

"Monkeys on the ground, people in the trees!" giggled his sisters.

"Monkeys on the ground, people in the trees, monkeys on the ground, people in the trees!" chanted his brothers, who began to dance again.

"Monkeys on the ground, people in the trees, monkeys on the ground, people in the trees!" chanted his sisters, joining the dance around the room.

John lost his temper. "You shut up!" he shouted at them.

That made them even madder at him. His sisters stuck out their tongues. His brothers stopped dancing.

"Re-tard! Re-tard!" they jeered at him.

John gave up again, and this time, instead of turning off the set, he switched channels back to the wrestling.

"Yaaaaay!" cheered his brothers and sisters.

John went to his mother, bending to speak directly into her ear. "Ma, I'm going on this trip tomorrow," he said. "You know, to see the whales. And I have to take a sack lunch."

She smiled and nodded, but didn't seem to understand. The wine made her that way.

"Ma, listen," he begged. "I have to take a sack lunch to school tomorrow."

Now she understood. "Sack lunch? What for? You're s'pose t'get your lunch at school."

"But I won't be in school tomorrow, remember? We're going on a trip."

She scowled. "Sack lunch? Sack lunch? I ain't makin' no sack lunch. You make your own!"

John went into the kitchen, which was dark because the lightbulb hanging from the ceiling had long ago burned out and had never been replaced. He scrounged

43

under the sink until he found a paper sack, then opened the refrigerator door. But the light was out in the refrigerator, too, so he had to kneel and feel from shelf to shelf. Finally he located a length of baloney, and shutting the door, got up and rummaged in a drawer for the knife. But there was none. It had to be in the sink with the dirty supper dishes. He clattered through them, found the knife, and was about to cut a slice or two of baloney when his mother entered the kitchen and in the dark, reaching for one of the wine bottles on the shelf, bumped into him.

"Who's that?" she cried, startled.

"It's me, Ma, John."

"What you doin'?"

"Making a sack lunch. You told me to."

"Sack lunch? What for?"

John sighed. "For school tomorrow."

"You s'pose t'get your lunch at school."

John gave up again. He said nothing, but cut two slices of baloney, being careful of his fingers. He knew where the bread was, and opening the wrapper took two slices, put the baloney between them, and stuck the sandwich in the paper sack.

She watched him. "You s'pose t'get your lunch at school. Well, ain't you?"

"Have some more wine, Ma," he said.

She slapped him.

"You got no cause t'talk t'your ma that way!" she cried. "I'll shut your mouth!"

For a moment John saw stars. He heard his mother's angry breathing. "I'm sorry, Ma," he said. "But I've

44

told you and told you. Our grade's going on a trip to-morrow, to see the whales. So we have to take sack lunches because we won't be at school, we'll be on a boat."

"You think you're so smart-ass," she accused. "Jus' 'cause you been t'school more'n I ever was. Well, you ain't. You're just a kid can't see straight or hear good. An' I'll tell you somethin' else. State has t'pay two hunnerd dollars a month for your schoolin'—they didn't have t'pay so much for you I might get more welfare! Ever think of that, huh? Your brothers an' sisters might have better clothes an' we might have more t'eat an' a color TV but for you! Sometimes I rue the day you was born, boy—you costin' the rest of us money!"

John didn't move.

"Whales?" she asked.

"Yes, Ma."

"Whales," she said in wonder. And then, unexpect-edly, almost knocking him down, she was on her knees with her arms around him, hugging him in the dark. "I never seen one. I'm glad you gonna." She was crying. Her tears were hot on his cheek. "I'm sorry, Johnny. Here." She released him, and seemed to be fumbling in a pocket of her dress. "Here. Gimme your hand." She put a coin in it. "There's a dime. Buy yourself somethin'. You have a good time."

"Thanks, Ma," he said.

She lumbered up and, sniffling, reached again for a bottle.

"Big day tomorrow. I better go to bed," he said. "Goodnight, Ma."

45

"Whales," she said.

Carrying coin and sack lunch, he went through the living room, where his brothers and sisters were still watching wrestling, and entering his mother's room, which she shared with his sisters, put the coin in her purse. It wasn't a dime. It was a nickel.

The phone rang in her apartment, and she answered it at once.

"Fish here." It was the way she always answered the telephone.

"Miss Sarah Fish?"

"That's correct."

"This is Cap'n Murphy, ma'am. You know, the one taking you and your kids to see the whales tomorrow?"

"Certainly."

"Sorry to call tonight, but I thought I'd better."

"Is anything wrong?"

"Well, ma'am, yes, there is. We cap'ns have to keep close track of the weather, so I called the Bureau tonight and it doesn't look good for tomorrow."

"Oh no. In what way?"

"High winds, ma'am. Which means high seas. And that's bad for two reasons. I'll have a boatful of sick kids, for one thing, and with the seas high, even if they weren't green around the gills they couldn't see whales."

"Oh no," said Miss Fish.

"The fact is, ma'am," Captain Murphy continued, "I called the Coast Guard, too, and they've put up small craft warnings. Which means small boats like mine ought not to be out."

"Mightn't the weather change?"

"It always does, sooner or later. But tomorrow isn't later. If you want my advice, ma'am, I'd put off your trip a day or two. I'm about to call Missus Bellows and tell her the same."

"Mrs. Bellows?"

"The other teacher, ma'am. The one keeping us company with her twenty."

Sarah Fish frowned into the phone as though the captain could see her. "Captain, let me get things straight. There will be another teacher aboard, with a class of twenty?"

"That's right, ma'am. Sixth-graders, too, just like yours."

"Dammit."

"Ma'am?"

"I thought we were to have your boat entirely to ourselves."

"Miss Fish, I'm sorry, but I have to make a living. Which means I have to sell tickets. Was I to take ten kids out every day I'd lose my boat. Your ten and Missus Bellows' twenty makes thirty, and that'll buy my oil."

"Mrs. Bellows. Are her children normal, do you know?"

"Normal?"

"That is, do they attend a regular school?"

"Far as I know, ma'am."

"Dammit."

"Why? Aren't yours normal?"

Miss Fish hesitated. "Of course they are. But they're also very special children."

47

"Oh. Well, ma'am, I surely wish you'd wait till this weather blows itself out."

"We can't," said Miss Fish.

"Can't? Why not?"

"They've already waited a month, and they can't wait another day. They're all ready, their sack lunches are packed, they'll scarcely sleep a wink tonight, I know. If I told them we must wait, Captain, they'd die!"

"Die?" Captain Murphy sounded suspicious. "Ma'am, did you say these are normal kids?"

"I did. But I also said they're very special, the dears. That's why we must go, we simply must."

The captain harrumphed. "Very well, ma'am. If you intend to go, I'll take you. But I've given you my best advice."

"You have and I'm grateful," said Miss Fish. "But I'm sure everything will be all right. You wait and see. The weather will change, the seas will be calm, the sun will shine, and we'll see more whales than you can shake a stick at. Leave it to the Lord, Captain. That's my advice to you."

"Ma'am," said he, "I'd rather leave it to the Weather Bureau." And he hung up on her.

"Well!" said Sarah Fish.

But when the phone rang at John's house, and his mother came into his room and said it was for him, and his brothers and sisters chanted, "It's a girl! It's a girl!" he didn't believe it. He had never had a telephone call from anyone in his life, nor had he ever called anyone. The reason they had a phone in the first place was

48

because his mother claimed she needed one to call ladies to see if she could get housework, but John noticed she never called anyone except her own friends, and then talked by the hour. He hadn't believed anyone would ever telephone him. But he put on his shoes and turned on his hearing aids and went into the living room. They had turned off the TV, and all five of them were standing around with their ears wiggling, just waiting to find out who it was and what he would say. John foxed them. The telephone sat on a table by a window. Raising the window, he placed the phone outside, on the windowsill, closed the window on top of the cord, went outside the house himself, and picked up the phone. His brothers and sisters made dumb faces and pressed their noses to the glass, but he knew they couldn't hear. He turned his back on them and swallowed several times.

"Hello?" he said.

"John?"

"Yes."

"Hello, John. This is Dee-Dee."

"Oh. Hi," he said.

"Hi," she said.

There was a pause. John had no idea what you were supposed to say over a telephone. "How are you?" he asked.

"Fine. How're you?"

"Okay."

There was another pause. "Do you use the telephone a lot?" he asked.

"Oh sure. All the time."

"Oh."

There was another pause. "You all ready for tomorrow?" he asked.

"Sure. Are you?"

"Sure."

There was another pause. "How come you called me?" he asked.

"Oh, I had a bad time with my folks tonight," she said. "At first I didn't think they'd let me go tomorrow, so I made up my mind. I had this plan. I was going to burn down our house."

"Burn down your house?"

"Yes. But then they said I could go, so I didn't."

"That's good."

There was another pause. "How come you called me?" he asked.

"To tell you something."

"What?"

"John, I think we ought to get married."

John almost dropped the phone. "Married?"

"Sure. Why not?"

"Why not? But why?"

"Well, I've been thinking," said Dee-Dee. "We've both got problems and we could help each other. I'm clumsy, and you could watch out for me. You don't hear well, and when your batteries go dead I could speak slowly and you could lip-read me."

"Oh."

"So I think we ought to get married."

"When?"

"Right away."

"Well, we can't tomorrow."

"I know that. But the sooner the better."

"But gee, we're pretty young."

"I know, but that's good. We can get away from our folks and be on our own and grow up together and it'll be great."

"But gosh, you're bigger than I am."

"Now I am. Girls always are at first. Later on you'll sprout up and your voice'll change and you'll grow a mustache or a beard or something."

"I will?" John said doubtfully. "But gee, I've got dyslexia and impaired hearing."

"So? I've got apraxia and hyperkinesia. So we're even."

"But gosh, we don't even know much about each other."

"I like to swim. I'm a terrific swimmer. Do you have any hobbies?"

"Well, I roll tires."

"Roll tires?"

"Down into a ravine. It's really neat."

"Oh. Well, okay, now we know all about each other. So what about it?"

"About what?"

"Getting married."

"Oh." John shivered. The night air was damp with fog even here, inland. "Well, listen, Dee-Dee, we better think this over. I mean, nobody's ever asked me to get married before, and it's pretty sudden. Let's talk about it tomorrow."

"Tomorrow!" For a moment she'd forgotten. "I can

hardly wait! John, honest, d'you really think we'll really see some?"

"Prob'ly not."

"Probably not? Don't be so—so negative." Dee-Dee was very proud of her vocabulary. "Why shouldn't we?"

"Because that's the way it always is."

"What always is?"

"I mean, you wait and wait for something and then nothing happens."

"Pooh. And sometimes it does, too, when you least expect it. Like tonight—did you ever dream I'd call you?"

"No."

"Well then. And maybe tomorrow—wow!"

"Maybe."

"I'd better get some shut-eye. Thanks for talking to me, John. Goodnight."

"Goodnight."

"Sleep tight and don't let the bugs bite."

"How'd you know?" he asked.

"Know what?"

"We've got bugs. Bedbugs."

"Ugh. You haven't."

"Yes, we do. And they do bite."

"Ugh. Well, we won't have any in our house after we're married."

"I better hit the sack," said John. "Goodnight, Dee-Dee. See you tomorrow."

"Goodnight, John. Dear."

Under the reaches of the sea the pod moved northward in the night. They moved in straight lines, and slowly, for the journey they must make was long beyond belief.

It had begun in the bays and coves of Lower California. Here they had mated and borne their young. Now, in spring, answering a call as old as earth, a summons only they could hear, they started north along the American coast. Night upon day, week upon month, they would swim eight thousand miles to the Bering Sea, and summer there in cold and windy waters. Then, in autumn, they would turn again to the south, to the sun, to the warm, to mate and bear their young and play and wait for that beckoning in the blood which would once more call them to the north.

There were forty or fifty in the pod. They swam beneath the surface of the sea, stroking up and down with their tails for seven or eight minutes. Then they surfaced and, "blowing," or opening and closing the nostril on top of their heads to empty and fill their great lungs, they "sounded" again, rolling over to dive again into darkness.

They traveled in family groups, bull, cow, and calf, father, mother, and child close by its mother and its "auntie," that cow without calf who tended the youngster as her own. As the forty or fifty traveled, they communicated by sounds, by barks, whistles, and calls under water, and by signals, by rolling and spinning, and by certain movements of the mouth, flippers, and flukes. Now and then a baby, assisted by its "auntie," would position itself near its mother's tail to nurse, and into its hungry mouth she would send jets of rich milk. Mother and child would rise to the surface afterward and, swimming side by side, touching, smack their blow-holes with contentment. Should they be separated from each other, so true and steadfast was their love that both would die.

Under the reaches of the sea the pod moved north-ward in the night. It needed no star to steer by. No storm or tide could turn it from its course. It was com-posed of living things which understood one another, of creatures which would guide and protect and care for one another until together, together, all had climbed the ocean to their journey's end.

three

Someone—probably another teacher—had stuck a bumper sticker on the Volkswagen bus that Miss Fish occasionally drove for the special school: HELL ON WHEELS. And she left it there, because she was. She two-wheeled the bus around corners. She tore through intersections on the yellow light. She ramped onto the freeway and drove lickety-split while Arnold and Anne and Sandra and Pablito and Myron and Musette and John and Ralph and Dee-Dee and Mike held onto their sack lunches and each other and stared out the windows at San Diego blurring by and hoped they'd get there in one piece.

They zipped around a camper, a sports car, and a cement mixer, and suddenly, shooting down an off-ramp like a torpedo, there they were, on the waterfront, and before they could collect their arms and legs and wits, Miss Fish had putzed into a parking space, slammed on the brakes, turned off the motor, and opened the door.

"Everybody out!" she whooped. "Don't forget your lunches, I'll give you your tickets, everybody stay together, look out, whales, here we come!"

She gave them each a ticket and herded her ten across the street and through a small, dark building and down some steps onto a dock, and suddenly, there they really were.

They stopped. They bumped into each other. They turned round and round like tops. There was so much to see they couldn't take it all in. There were oily waters and seagulls and cranes and on one side the huge hull of a Japanese freighter loading spools of copper cable from the dock into its holds, with its name in large letters on its bow—*Chicago Maru*—and on the other side of the dock was *The Protector*. Could that possibly be their boat? That?

"No kidding," blurted Ralph. "We going on that?"

"On the ocean?" worried Musette.

"I've got a bigger boat right at home!" cracked Myron, the class clown. "In the bathtub!"

Compared to the Japanese freighter, *The Protector* was practically dinky. She was sixty-five feet long and sixteen feet wide. Her hull was white, her cabin and bridge and wheelhouse and the letters of her name were orange, and her funnel was striped white-and-orange. She was old, too, having been built in 1944 and used for many years by the Boston Police Department as a harbor boat—which was how she got her name, *The Protector*. But what the children couldn't know was that Captain Murphy, who had bought her in 1962 and sailed her all the way from Boston through the Panama Canal to San Diego, had refitted her completely, top to bottom. She was now powered by two 300-horsepower diesel engines, with twin throttles on the bridge and two

56

propellers at the stern. With a stern breeze they could push her fourteen knots an hour. He had also installed a depth recorder, to tell him how much water he had under him, an automatic direction finder, to tell him which way to go if he got lost, and a radar with a fifteen-mile range, so that in the fog he wouldn't run into a jaywalker or a telephone pole. He had even bought himself a long-distance, high-frequency, ship-to-shore radio transmitter, in case he wanted to call Australia and ask how the kangaroos were.

"Morning, boys and girls. Morning, Miss Fish." It was Captain Murphy, standing on the bridge like the master of the *Queen Elizabeth II* and tipping his cap. "You may bring them aboard now. Have them give their tickets to my crew."

"What crew?" she asked, looking about.

"Why, Tony there."

He nodded at a skinny young man of twenty or so who stood by the gangway combing his long black hair and being bored. He wore blue bellbottoms and a white T-shirt with EAT YOUR HEARTS OUT, GIRLS! on the front. Tony spent a great deal of time combing his hair because he expected soon to be a movie star.

And up the gangway went Miss Fish's class, handing their tickets to Tony. They stowed sack lunches in the cabin, which had tables and benches and a water cooler, and lifejackets lashed to the ceiling, and had just come out on deck again, when there, on the dock, facing them, holding sack lunches, tickets ready, and about to board, were twenty other boys and girls their own age and a very large, teachery-looking woman.

"Don't stare, children," said Miss Fish. "I understand we're to have another class of sixth-graders with us today. After all, we can't expect to have the whole boat to ourselves, can we?"

"Why? Not?" demanded Mike.

Miss Fish ignored him. "Now line up by the cabin door and take your pills, please. Dee-Dee, John, you be in charge. Here are paper cups, and each one's name is on his pill bottle. One apiece, come along, step lively."

She hoped to have the pill taking over by the time the stranger children boarded, but it was too late now. The other class was filing up the gangway and staring at her class, lined up and drinking and swallowing and making faces.

The other teacher bore down on Miss Fish like an ocean liner bearing down on a tug. "Good morning, you must be Miss Fish." She extended a hand.

"I certainly am." Miss Fish took the hand and got a grip of iron. "And you must be Mrs. Bellows."

"Nobody else! Captain Murphy mentioned you when he called last night about the weather. How nice to have another teacher and class aboard, so we can all get to know each other."

"Yes, isn't it?" smiled Miss Fish, who observed just then that Pablito was making donkey's-ears at the new arrivals, and that Sandra was crossing her eyes and sticking out her tongue.

"I see your children are taking pills," said Mrs. Bellows. "Are they seasick pills? How thoughtful of you to bring some along."

Miss Fish considered saying yes, but she didn't be-

58

lieve in telling large lies. Little lies were perfectly permissible, she felt, but whoppers never. "Well, no, they aren't," she admitted.

"They aren't? What are they, then?"

"Well, each child of mine is under different medication, prescribed by a doctor."

"By a doctor?"

"Yes. Some take suppressants, some stimulants, and some tranquilizers."

Mrs. Bellows was amazed. "Stimulants? Suppressants? What in the world's the matter with them?"

"Nothing's the matter," said Miss Fish rather sharply. "It's just that they're very special children. Oh, excuse me, please. Some of them are misbehaving." And she went quickly to Pablito and Sandra to tell them to stop and to tell Dee-Dee and John to hurry up the pills.

"C'mon, you kids," said Dee-Dee. "Last one gets pushed overboard and drownded." And she tossed a pill into her mouth and washed it down.

"Drowned," corrected Miss Fish.

"Down the hatch," said John, and popped his into his mouth. But before he could raise his paper cup, a horn on the funnel blasted, making everyone jump, and John swallowed his pill dry, choked, and had to be pounded on the back.

They were sailing!

Tony stuck his comb in his pocket, pushed the gangway away from the side, sprang onto the deck, dropped in a length of rail to fill the gap, ran forward, cast off the bow line, ran aft, cast off the stern line, and waved at the bridge, where Captain Murphy stood in the

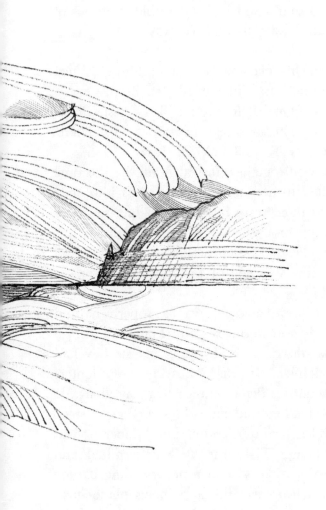

wheelhouse at the throttles. The engines growled below decks, propellers spun the oily water into foam, and *The Protector* moved backward and away from the dock.

"Hooray!" shouted the thirty children.

"Hooooooooray!" shouted Sarah Fish.

No one noticed that a stiff breeze had blown in out of the west, and that the day had turned gray.

Mike gathered his classmates around him. "Listen. You. Guys," he said with difficulty. "I've. Been. On. A. Boat. Like. This. Once. Before. And. The. Best. Place. To. See. From. Is. The. Bow. So. Let's. Get. Up. There. Before. Those. Other. Kids. Think. Of. It!"

And off they went together, forward, and by the time *The Protector* had turned around and started into open water, the ten of them were lined up shoulder-to-shoulder in the bow, five on each side. Mike was right. It was indeed the best place to be on a sightseeing boat. And what they saw now was one of the great sights on an American coast.

The bay they were crossing was a superb natural harbor. Protected from storm by Point Loma, an arm of land, so that its waters were always calm, the bay had many coves and inlets. It was a busy port. Freighters from faraway countries flying strange flags lay alongside a mile of docks, loading and unloading cargoes of steel, radios, automobiles, fertilizer, cotton, and lumber. It was also next to Lindbergh Field, the city's air terminal, and to a Coast Guard station, so that a never-ending parade of jetliners and helicopters and amphibious planes took off and landed, roaring overhead. It was also one of the largest bases of the United States Navy. They passed two giant gray aircraft carriers, the *Kitty Hawk* and the *Ticonderoga,* their decks alive with crewmen and heavy with fighter planes, wings folded. They passed a cruiser, a guided-missile frigate, six destroyer escorts, several landing transports, supply ships, and minesweepers. In one cove was the "mothball fleet," moored row upon row, ghostly warships from the Second World War, their portholes covered, their guns plugged, moored at rest but ready to be refitted and to prowl the seas again if need should be. They passed a brood of submarines, one of them a nuclear sub, nestled up to a "mother ship" like chicks to a hen. On one spit of land was a naval air station. Radar planes were sent from here to patrol the California coastline, and Navy pilots never ceased to practice take-offs and landings. The harbor was alive with tugs, lighters, barges, and pleasure craft, darting and veering, and even an admiral's gig, a speedboat with two sailors in dress whites standing aft and a blue flag with white stars whipping. Finally, there was the scope and beauty of the entire scene to marvel at—the tall buildings of downtown San Diego backed by wooded hills, the highland to the north, massed with houses in the suburbs of La Jolla and Mission Beach, and to the south the arch of the Coronado Bridge and the silver strand of sand curving out of sight, an arm beckoning to Tijuana and the border of Old Mexico.

Lined up shoulder-to-shoulder, five at the rail on each side of the bow, Miss Fish's ten gaped. And gawked. And goggled.

Moving about the decks, looking first at this, then at

63

that, Mrs. Bellows' twenty youngsters happened naturally to gather in the bow, for that was the best place to
see. But they found their view blocked.

"Hey, you guys," said one, a boy named Todd, "how
about changing places for a while?"

No one in the bow moved a muscle.

"How about it?" Todd repeated. "Everybody should
have a chance—it's only fair."

"We got here first," said Arnold.

"But that's childish."

"Are you kids on drugs?" asked a girl named Gloria.
"I mean, what were those pills? Seasick pills?"

No one in the bow said word one.

"Say, what's the matter with you?" asked Gloria im-
patiently. "We're all in the same boat, and we will be
all day. How come you're so stuck-up?"

She was interrupted. "Well, young ladies and gents,
I hope you're enjoying the sights of San Diego."

It was the voice of Captain Murphy, speaking into a
loudspeaker system on the bridge.

"Now I want to tell you something about why we're
here today and what we're going to do," he continued.
"Depending on the weather, of course," he added. "We
are going out to see some gray whales if we can. We'll
be out of the harbor soon, pass Point Loma, and set sail
upon the briny deep. We'll proceed south by southwest
about nine miles, to the Coronado Islands. You might see
some seals on the rocks there, but that's not what we're
going for. We hope to see whales, as many as we can, and
you ought to know a few things about 'em before we
get there. So I'll just ramble on and you listen when you

64

feel like it. Now the gray whale is the oldest of all the whales—what you might call a living fossil. It is a mammal, too. By that I mean a mother whale will bear a live baby and nurse him. But what he's got to have first is a breath of air, as we all do. So what she does —his mother—as soon as he's born, she swims under him and nuzzles him up and up to the surface till whuff!—he opens his baby blowhole on top of his head and gets a good whiff. Now what d'you think of that?"

Todd and Gloria found Mrs. Bellows at the stern, where the two propellers, spinning, spread a white wash of wake behind *The Protector*. Seagulls followed her, hovering overhead and screaming for handouts.

"Mrs. Bellows, what kind of pills were those other kids taking?" Gloria wanted to know.

"Well, I'm not really sure, dear. I know they're not seasick pills. I asked their teacher myself, but all she'd say was that each one of her class takes a particular kind of pill, prescribed by a doctor."

"A doctor?"

"What's with them, anyway?" Todd asked. "They're really a freak outfit. They stick together in the bow and won't give any of us a chance—talk about selfish. Is there something wrong with 'em?"

"Todd, I don't know," said Mrs. Bellows, choosing her words carefully. "Miss Fish, their teacher, simply said they were very special children."

"Special? I'll say they are," said Gloria scornfully.

"My guess—my guess is that they're handicapped in some way."

"Oh," said Todd. "Well, they can be handicapped,

but they don't have to be cruddy."

"Now one reason why we're lucky to live in California is that, if we want to, we can watch whales every year—twice a year, in fact." It was Captain Murphy again, over the loudspeakers. "And the reason is that gray whales make a long journey every year up and down our coast. Eight thousand miles they travel, each way. They spend the summer way up north, off Alaska, in the Bering Sea, where they can keep cool as cucumbers. And they spend the winter down south of us here, in the bays of Baja California, where they can keep warm and get a fine tan. So to be comfortable, winter and summer, they have to travel back and forth, south in the fall and north in the spring. This being March, if I'm not mistaken, they're on their way to the Bering Sea. It's called a 'migration.' They travel night and day and never stop to have a bite to eat or anything—unlike some youngsters I know. And what we hope to do is see some of 'em migrating north today, just cruising along like they're on a freeway. Except whales never get off at the wrong ramp or run out of gas or have a flat tire."

"That captain," scoffed Myron. "He thinks he's a comedian."

No one noticed that a stiff breeze had blown in out of the west, and that the day had grown gray.

Hoisting himself with his elbows up on the rail, which wasn't very high, John stared downward, fascinated by the split and splash of water rushing along the bow.

"Do you really think we'll see some?" asked Dee-Dee,

who stood close beside him.

"Prob'ly not."

"There you go again—I told you, don't be so negative." She stood even closer and spoke into his hearing aid. "John, have you been thinking about what I said last night?"

"About what?"

"About getting married, stupo."

"Oh. That."

"Well?"

"Well, gee, I don't know," John said. "Hey, look at that water, though, the way the bow tickles it and it laughs foam."

"Don't change the subject."

"How'd we make a living?"

"A living?"

"You know, buy groceries and pay the rent and stuff like that."

Dee-Dee frowned, thinking. "Well, you're the man, you're supposed to get out and work and support us. What can you do?"

"I told you—roll tires."

"Maybe you could do that on television and make pots of money."

"Maybe." John was doubtful. "I don't think so, though."

She had a bright idea. "I know—we'd live on our allowances. I get two dollars a week—how much do you get?"

"Nothing."

"Nothing? You're kidding."

"No, I'm not. My mother's on welfare."

"Oh. Well, what about your father?"

"I don't have one. I mean, I must have had one once, but he left when I was little. I've never heard of him since."

"Oh, John, that's too bad."

"So we couldn't live on our allowances."

"I guess not."

"And besides that, where would we live?"

"Why, at your house, of course. You'd be the husband. I'd bring over my radio and TV and records and clothes and things and we'd have your room."

John grinned. Dee-Dee couldn't remember ever seeing him do that before. "My room, sure. Swell. If you wouldn't mind sharing the bed with two others besides me."

"Two others?"

"My little brothers. They sleep with me and have bad dreams and yell and kick me out on the floor. How'd you like to be kicked out on the floor every night?"

Dee-Dee looked at him, then grew angry and stuck out her chin. "John, you just keep putting up objections. You're impossible—all boys are impossible."

"We are?"

"Yes. Because you're so—so—immature."

"We'll soon be passing Point Loma and be out in open water. So now, young gents and ladies, I'll say a last few words about the gray whales," continued Captain Murphy over the loudspeaker. "A full-grown gray whale is forty to fifty feet long and weighs thirty to forty tons. If you can't picture anything that big, just imagine a Greyhound bus swimming around. A gray whale is harmless and can be approached quite closely by boat. It feeds mostly from the bottom of the sea on little shellfish no bigger than your fingernail. And a gray whale is very human. It gets sick and has accidents and things wrong with it sometimes—just like most of us. Its two worst enemies are killer whales, which attack it and tear it apart and eat its tongue, and man. By the year 19 and 24 it was almost wiped out by man, hunting it for its oil and bones and things. But now, I'm glad to say, whaling agreements between countries protect it, so that the gray whale population is back up to about ten thousand. Well, that's the end of my story, young ladies and gents. I wish we could see all ten thousand of 'em, but of course we can't. Anyway, we'll see some, I hope. Depending on the weather. Good luck and thank you for listening."

While all the children were out on deck, Miss Fish and Mrs. Bellows met by chance in the cabin. Each had come to be certain her class's sack lunches were properly stowed, and found they were, ten at one end on a bench, twenty at the other.

"I think the captain's lecture has been very valuable, don't you, Miss Fish?"

"I do. My class knows a great deal about the gray whale, though. We've been reading about them and getting ready for this trip for a whole month."

"I see. How nice. Well, we take so many trips we just don't have much time for preparation." Mrs. Bellows sat down on a bench. "Have you been teaching

69

long, Miss Fish?"

"Forty years this year."

"Forty years! Oh, my goodness. You are a trooper!"

"And you, Mrs. Bellows?"

"Just eight. Ever since my own children were grown enough for high school. I have two, a boy and a girl. You know how that goes—suddenly they're gone every day and the house is lonely and you simply must do something."

"I'm sure," replied Miss Fish.

"Have you children?"

"Just my ten. I never married."

"Oh. What a pity." Mrs. Bellows folded mighty arms across a mighty chest. "Miss Fish, I hope you don't mind my asking, but I'm curious. And so are my children— it was the drugs. You told me your class is very special. Do you mind my asking—are they handicapped?"

Miss Fish sat down herself. She thought for a minute, while belowdecks the two engines made a hot and diesel racket. "I guess there's no harm in telling you, Mrs. Bellows," she said at last. "It was bound to come up anyway —if not between us, then between our classes. It always does, unfortunately. Children have a way of finding out about each other, and they can be very cruel. Yes, they're handicapped. My children are neurologically impaired."

Mrs. Bellows was shocked. "What a shame." She shook her head. "I'm so sorry."

"Don't be," said Miss Fish tartly. "Sympathy won't help, I've found. What they need is understanding."

Mrs. Bellows frowned. "There's one thing I don't understand. When Captain Murphy called me last night,

70

he said you insisted on taking your class today regardless of the weather and his advice. Why would you do that?"

"Because they've been planning on it for a month, and I couldn't bear to disappoint them. Children like mine miss out on so many things anyway, and I—"

"But if it should get stormy, even dangerous," interrupted Mrs. Bellows. "I wouldn't think of taking mine out in a small boat like this—and they're not handicapped, they're quite normal. I told the captain that if the weather were really bad, I'd expect him to turn back and wait for—"

Miss Fish sat up straight. "Oh no, we can't do that. We—"

"Why in heaven's name not?"

"Because my boys and girls simply must see the whales. They've waited—"

"At the risk of their lives?" It was Mrs. Bellows' turn to sit up straight. "I'm sorry, Miss Fish. I sympathize with your children, but I cannot and will not endanger my—"

Now she was interrupted. Both teachers heard a loud chanting outside the cabin, near the bow. It was the same word, over and over: "Re-tards! Re-tards!" Both teachers were on their feet in a flash, peering through the cabin windows.

"Oh no!" lamented Miss Fish.

"Absolutely not!" cried Mrs. Bellows.

"Re-tards! Re-tards!" shouted Mrs. Bellows' twenty. Their anger at being denied the bow, the best sightseeing place on the boat, had finally boiled over, and now they stood in a gang, shouting the worst word they could think of at Miss Fish's ten.

Pablito and Anne and John and Musette and Arnold and Dee-Dee and Ralph and Myron and Mike and Sandra kept their backs turned at first, pretending not to hear. But finally the chant became so loud that they had to do something. It was the worst word they knew, too. They had heard it almost from the first day they had ever gone to school, spat and whispered and shouted at them by other boys and girls. Sometimes it was "M.R.! M.R.!" for "mentally retarded," or "Freak! Freak!" but whatever the word, the meaning was the same. It had followed them through every grade, through every defeat and embarrassment and bad report card and every broken friendship, until they were enrolled in special school. They had heard it in class, at recess, after school, and on the weekends. They had heard it at work, at play, and in their sleep. It was the word they hated and feared above every other in the language.

"Re-tards! Re-tards!" chorused Mrs. Bellows' twenty.

In his mind's eye, John saw two tires racing down the side of the ravine, across the bottom, rushing at the wall of the other side, and trying, trying to climb it. That they never made it didn't matter. The important thing was that they tried. And one day, he knew, one wonderful day, all by themselves they would.

Like a rolling tire he rushed at the biggest boy in the other class, the boy named Todd, and, swinging a fist, aimed it at Todd's chin. He missed, and hit Todd a glancing blow on the shoulder.

Todd swung in return, instinctively, and struck John squarely in the mouth. John went down sprawling.

Dee-Dee saw him go down. With a wail like a siren she left her place and tore into Todd, banging him around the head and shoulders with her fists.

Gloria attempted to haul her away from Todd, but Dee-Dee turned and, getting her hands in Gloria's hair, gave it a good hard pull.

That set the rest off like a string of firecrackers. The boys, Mike and Arnold and Ralph and Pablito and Myron, charged at the boys in the other class, while Anne, Sandra, and Musette attacked the girls.

In seconds the bow was a barrel of monkeys, a welter of furious youngsters hitting and slapping and wrestling and crying and wondering secretly why the dickens they were hitting and slapping and wrestling and crying.

Then Miss Fish was in the middle of it, trying to separate fighters and pleading, "Oh no, dear children, you mustn't, you simply mustn't—please, please!"

Then Mrs. Bellows waded in with might and main, tugging and jerking and bellowing, "Absolutely not! Now you stop this, or I'll take you all over my knees and whale the living tar out of you!"

But the battle ended suddenly.

For suddenly both teachers and both classes shot up, up, up into the air while their stomachs dropped down, down, down!

Then both teachers and both classes dropped down, down, down while their stomachs shot up, up, up into the air!

The Protector had passed Point Loma.

She was out of San Diego harbor now, and into open water.

Not one among her passengers had ever imagined what an ocean could do to a small boat when it wanted to. The breeze which had blown in unnoticed out of the west while they were in port had become a fierce wind sweeping the decks like a broom. Clouds swung across the sky like doors closing, and the gray day had become almost black. But it was what the wind could do to the waves and the waves could do to *The Protector* that frightened everyone out of a year's growth. Up the side of one massive wave she lifted, crested, hung an instant, then slid down into a trough between waves so high that they blotted out the land and the sky. Her bow smashed into the oncoming waves with a crash, showering spray over the decks. And while her bow was down, her stern was entirely out of water, so that the twin propellers turned in air, vibrating, shivering her timbers from end to end. Then her bow went up, pointed at the sky, and her stern fell and the propellers bit into water like a dog into a bone. This motion sailors call "pitching."

The winds and seas, however, had still another trick up their sleeves. Since *The Protector* could make only slow headway against the waves, sometimes she wallowed sideways in a trough, the masses of water tipping her to one side on their upward thrust, then tipping her to the other on the downward—tipping her so far that everyone was certain she would turn upside down, capsize, and sink like a stone—tipping her so far that the edges of her decks were awash with icy, salty rivers. This motion sailors call "rolling."

Boys, girls, and teachers reeled and staggered and grabbed any grabbable—rails, cabin walls, and each other—and held on for dear life. The eyes of some bulged in terror as they beheld the terrible waves march toward them like armies. The eyes of others closed, their lips moved, and they seemed to be praying.

"Now young ladies and gents, everybody, this is Captain Murphy again," the loudspeaker soothed. "Have no fear. *The Protector* is thirty years old—old enough to know what she's doing and take care of herself. We only have six miles to go to the Coronados. I doubt we'll see any whales on a day like this—I doubt they'll see us either—but you'll get your sea legs in an hour or two and be just fine and dandy."

The loudspeaker clicked off. The captain's words had reassured nobody.

"In an hour or two?" said everyone. "An hour or two of this?"

And then a quavery voice was raised in song. It was Myron, the class clown, singing "Many Brave Hearts Are Asleep in the Deep."

They tried to laugh, but something was happening to them now that was even worse than the weather. They began to turn every color of the rainbow, although most favored blue and green. And suddenly, almost on signal, everyone reeled to the rails and started to urp. They were completely and utterly and totally seasick. And

75

when you are truly seasick, you are as sick as you ever care to be. You feel you might die, and fear that you won't, for death, you would swear on a stack of Bibles, would be better than this. The children groaned and moaned and urped—over the rails, on the decks, over each other. Tony, the crew, got out his bucket and brush and went along the rails swabbing urp into the sea, grinning at everyone and stopping now and then to comb his movie-star hair.

Miss Fish refused to be seasick. I am sixty-two years old and a prim and proper spinster, she said to herself, and if I didn't push the panic button yesterday, I will not be seasick today. I must set a good example for these children, and I must attend to them in whatever way I can.

There wasn't much, however, she could do. She held their heads over the rail, she mopped their faces, she patted and petted them, but sick they were and sick they continued to be.

Ill though he was, Myron tried to be funny. "Time for lunch!" he bawled. "Anybody hungry?"

They wailed at him, and at the thought of food were sicker than ever.

"Sardines," groaned John. "If I could just quit thinking about—"

"I feel awful!" moaned Dee-Dee.

"If I could just quit, period," groaned John. "We won't see any whales—I knew it. I'm going up and tell that dumb captain to turn this tub around."

"You're what? John, you can't!"

"Heck I can't!"

76

Dee-Dee was shocked as well as sick, but not surprised. Just as John could turn his hearing aids and himself off and be stubborn for hours, he could turn himself on again and do whatever weird thing he wanted to.

"I'm going with you!" she cried.

He shook his head. "We're not married yet!" And pushing himself away from the rail he started aft, toward the bridge, Dee-Dee tagging after him.

Mrs. Bellows also refused to give in to minor things like rolling and pitching and winds and oceans. If that little old contraption of a teacher can stay well and strong, she said to herself, so can I, and I shall. I shall set a good example for my class and help them in any way I can.

There wasn't much, however, she could do. She held their heads over the rails, she mopped their faces, she patted and petted them, but sick they were and sick they continued to be.

"Oh, Mrs. Bellows," moaned Gloria. "I feel awful!"

"So do I!" groaned Todd. "But let's not make a big deal out of it! This probably builds character!"

"Character!" moaned Gloria. "Mrs. Bellows, can't we please, please go back?"

"Well," said her teacher, "I did tell the captain last night—if the weather was bad I'd expect him to turn back and take us out another day! I'd go up and have it out with him right now—but I could never climb that little ladder!"

"I can!" cried Gloria. "Is it okay if I go up there and tell him you want us to go home?"

Mrs. Bellows considered, then made up her mind, Miss

Fish and her ten handicapped children notwithstanding. "Yes, you can!" she shouted. "You go right ahead, Gloria!"

Gloria tried to stand, lurched, and might have fallen had Todd not caught her. "I'm going with you!"

"Why?"

"Because I'm not in favor—I'm not a quitter! I want to hear what that captain says!"

She really didn't mind his coming, and so, clutching each other, they made a teetery way aft, to the forward bulkhead of the cabin. But when they reached the foot of the steep, narrow ladder which led above the cabin to the bridge, a smallish boy with glasses was already climbing it, followed closely by an awkward girl who was trying to haul him back down by the shirt. Gloria started up, too, and Todd as well.

"Lemme go!" yelled John.

"You can't do this!" cried Dee-Dee.

"Out of my way, you two!" cried Gloria.

"What is this—King of the Hill?" yelled Todd over the keening of the wind and the rush of the waters. "Let's go—everybody up!"

The four moved again, clutching the brass handrail on each side. Near the top, John made the mistake of stopping for one last look below, and so did Dee-Dee, and so did Gloria. So scary was it that none of them could budge.

"Move it!" yelled Todd, and charged upward at Gloria like a football player.

Gloria butted Dee-Dee and Dee-Dee bumped into John and John flew onto the bridge, seized the doorknob,

flung open the door, and all four of them boomed into the wheelhouse like cannonballs.

"Why, good morning, young ladies and gents," said Captain Murphy, tipping his cap.

"Good morning, Captain," said Dee-Dee, giving him the benefit of her smiliest smile.

"Good morning, I guess," offered Gloria.

"Hi, Skipper," said Todd, closing the wheelhouse door.

"Good morning my foot," said John. "What is this—a tropical typhoon?"

"Just a stiff blow," the captain assured him, keeping both hands on the wheel. "Well, now you're here, have a look round, all of you."

The four crowded the windows. The view from the wheelhouse was even more terrifying than it had been from the ladder. *The Protector* seemed to them no larger, or safer, than a rowboat. Their friends, clinging to the rails below, looked like helpless infants. And the wheelhouse itself seemed no more than a leaf on a tree in a storm, trembling, tossing this way and that, rising and falling, controlled by forces more powerful than mere man could measure. Now all they could see was sea. Now all they could see was sky. Now and then they caught a glimpse, on the far horizon ahead, of dark knobs jutting from the angry waters.

"That's the Coronados," Captain Murphy told them. "Another hour away, I'd reckon. We can't make much more than two, three knots on a bumpy road like this.

Don't know why the city of San Diego hasn't paved it by now."

"Holy smoly," groaned John. "You mean we have to urp another hour yet?"

"I expect so," agreed the captain.

Todd was inspecting the machinery—the dials and gauges and scopes of the depth recorder, the direction finder, the black boxes of the radio receiver and transmitter, the twin throttles which regulated the speed of the engines.

"Well, well," said the captain, "we have company." He pointed. "That'll be the Coast Guard."

Off the port beam a silvery helicopter sped toward them several hundred feet above the water, its rotating blades a shimmer. Closer and closer it skimmed, then slowed to hover almost directly above *The Protector*. By craning heads, the four youngsters could make out the silhouette of the pilot, and the red-and-white striping on the craft which signified U. S. Coast Guard.

"He'll be wanting a word with us," said the captain, flicking a switch on his receiver and tuning to the right wavelength.

The box squawked, then cleared, and a young voice said, *"Protector,* what the devil you doing out in weather like this with all those kids? Over."

Captain Murphy flicked another switch, bent down, and spoke into the transmitter. "Why, we're going out to see the whales, laddie."

"Whales? In weather like this?"

"If they don't mind it, we don't," replied the captain briskly.

"Ha-ha," responded the pilot. "Well, if you need any help, let us know. Over."

"We will. And if you need any, give us a whistle," said the captain, winking at his guests. "Over and out."

The pilot waved, and the chopper droned away like a bee.

"Young whippersnapper," said the captain, switching off his boxes. "And now, you four, why don't you introduce yourselves."

They looked at each other. Two were strangers to the other two, and shy, and suspicious, and no one knew how to begin.

"I'm Dee-Dee."

"I'm Gloria."

"I'm Todd."

"I'm dying," said John.

"Pleased to make your acquaintance," smiled Captain Murphy. "And what can I do for you this fine morning?"

Gloria came to the point. "My teacher, Mrs. Bellows, asked me to come tell you she thinks we should go home. And we do, too, all the kids in her class."

"That's a smart class," said John. "I knew all along— we're not going to see any—"

"Well, my teacher, Miss Fish, would have a hissy if we went back now," Dee-Dee declared. "And so would I. We want to keep going and—"

"Not me," John interrupted.

"John, you hush," Dee-Dee warned.

"You can say anything you want, John," Gloria glared at Dee-Dee.

"No, he can't," Dee-Dee glared at Gloria. "You don't

know him. He's a very negative person, and—"

"Wait a second, everybody simmer down," Todd broke in, gripping the radarscope with a hand to keep his balance. "Skipper, what do you think?" he asked the captain. "You're the only one who knows the score."

Captain Murphy ran a finger round his shirt collar. "Well, the fact is, we are in no danger from the weather. This boat of mine has stood up to much worse. But it's also a fact that when we do get out to the Coronados, with seas this high we can't possibly see any whales. You need a nice day for that, and—"

"There," said Gloria.

"That does it," said John.

"But mightn't the weather change?" Dee-Dee appealed.

"It might," the captain admitted. "It always does, sooner or later. But I don't see any break now, young miss, so unless we have a miracle—"

"There," said Gloria.

"That does it," said John.

"Chickens," said Dee-Dee.

"I'd rather be a live chicken than a dead duck," said John.

"I'm with you," Todd said to Dee-Dee. "I hate to give up on anything. I think we ought to tough it out and take our chances. Who knows, maybe—"

"Who believes in miracles any more?" sniffed Gloria.

"Well now there, I don't know," said Captain Murphy. "I've been to sea a long time, and I've seen many a strange sight. Have a look at this." He pointed to a small white card thumbtacked up by one of the windows above the wheel, a card with five lines of typing on it. "Read it," he advised. "I do, every day."

The four crowded around the wheel and leaned to scan these lines:

> *They that go down to the sea in ships,*
> *That do business in great waters;*
> *These see the works of the Lord,*
> *And His wonders in the deep.*
>
> *Psalms 107:23–24*

"So?" said Gloria.

"I think it's beautiful," sighed Dee-Dee. "Just like a poem. Don't you, John?"

"How do I know?" said John. "I had sardines for breakfast, and—"

"I think it's great," said Todd, nodding at Dee-Dee. "And I get the message. We've got to—"

"We're just spinning our wheels!" cried Gloria. "There are twenty in our class and we want to go back and there's only ten in yours, so it's two to one. I'm sorry, but we can't help it if you're handicapped and never go anywhere. And anyway, Mrs. Bellows said—"

"What's that?" Captain Murphy bent forward suddenly, over the wheel. "What's going on down there?"

Dee-Dee and Todd and Gloria and John clustered at the windows. Below them, on the foredeck, the two classes faced each other, some standing, some sitting on the deck, some grasping the rails. Seasick though the youngsters were, the expressions of hatred on their pale faces were as obvious as they had been earlier in the voyage, just before John attacked Todd and started the general fight. There were shouts, the words blown away. Several of Miss Fish's class were crying, tears streaming down their cheeks, while several others pointed at something in the sea.

What they pointed at was sack lunches—ten of them tossing on the waves—a small flotilla of food floating past *The Protector* as she rolled and pitched and drew away from them.

Someone—undoubtedly someone in Mrs. Bellows' class —had sneaked them out of the cabin and thrown them overboard.

Meanwhile, just entering the cabin, the two teachers were having their own hammer-and-tongs discussion.

"It's too late to argue," said Mrs. Bellows. "I've sent one of my girls, Gloria, to tell the captain I expect him to take us back at once."

"You haven't!" protested Miss Fish. "Without even consulting me?"

Mrs. Bellows cheeks reddened with exasperation. "I'm sorry, Miss Fish, but I have just as much responsibility to my class and my parents as you do to yours. And I don't intend for the sake of ten handicapped—"

"But mightn't your children learn something by sticking it out?" asked Miss Fish, turning pink herself.

"And I love mine just as much as you love yours— maybe more! I'm a mother myself, don't forget—and you're not and never have been!"

"Please, Mrs. Bellows," begged Sarah Fish. "I haven't meant to hurt you—don't hurt me."

"Hurt you? How can I? You're incapable of being

hurt!" cried Mrs. Bellows. "There's something wrong with you, too—you're just as abnormal as your children!"

"Oh no!" cried Sarah Fish, but not at the other teacher. She had just seen, out a cabin window, what Dee-Dee and John and Gloria and Todd had seen from the wheelhouse above—ten sack lunches bobbing past *The Protector* as she rolled and pitched and drew away from them. "Dammit!" she cried. "They shouldn't have done that!"

Mrs. Bellows followed her gaze through the window and was struck, for once, speechless. When she regained her voice, it was broken. "Oh, Miss Fish," she murmured, "I am so ashamed. What a cruel, dreadful thing—and one of mine must have done it." Her eyes were wet, and she turned her head. "I apologize."

"Don't, my dear," said Miss Fish. "It isn't the loss of the lunches—they're too sick to eat anyway. What I'm sorry about is the hatred between our children, the lack of understanding, and—" She had an idea. "Mrs. Bellows, will you do something for me—or let me try something? Something which should be tried before we throw in the towel and turn back?"

Mrs. Bellows found a Kleenex in her sleeve and gave her nose a good honk. "Yes, anything."

"Will you assemble your class in here and let me say a few words to them? And then, if they still want to return to port, I'll put up no further objections."

"Of course I will, of course you may—I'm so ashamed." Mrs. Bellows blew her nose again. "I'll assemble them at once."

"I'll be here," said Sarah Fish. "Waiting."

She stood at the bow end of the cabin while Mrs. Bellows rounded up her twenty and herded them in and sat them on benches and closed the door and stood guard by it, arms folded across her chest. The twenty boys and girls were clearly reluctant to come in or sit down or be lectured by anyone, particularly an old-maid teacher. They were blue and green and sick and guilty. One of them—they knew not who—had heaved the lunches into the drink, and while it served the re-tards right, the deed discredited them all. And so, as the wind clawed at the cabin and *The Protector*'s hull and bulkheads creaked, they squirmed and scowled and stared out the windows and wished they were off this urpy boat and home playing or watching TV or anything, even doing homework.

Oh, how will I ever, ever find the right words? thought Sarah Fish. How can I ever, ever make them understand? But I must, or everything's gone gaflooey.

Anne and Sandra's heads appeared at a window. They were dying to see what was going on in the cabin.

Just then Miss Fish had another idea. Instead of standing here like a ninny and nattering at them, I'll start it another way, she thought, I'll get them involved before they know it. That's it, by jingo! So come on, Sarah girl, open your mouth and see what comes out!

"Thank you so much," she began. "I'm so sorry the weather's bad today, and I know just how wretched you must feel. I also know you must be very curious about the other ten boys and girls aboard *The Protector* today.

Well, they're sixth-graders, just like you, at a special school in San Diego, and I'm their teacher. My name is Sarah Fish."

Someone stifled a snicker.

"You've noticed something different about them, I'm sure," she continued. "Everyone does. And there must be some questions you'd like to ask me—so please do. Feel free to ask anything you like, and I promise I'll answer truthfully. Well? Does anyone have a question?"

No one did. They scuffed their shoes and wiggled. That's it, she thought. The game hasn't even started, and I've already struck out.

Pablito peered into a cabin window.

But then a girl spoke up. It was Gloria. "What were those pills they took?"

Miss Fish could have hugged her. "I'm so glad you asked, my dear. They are pills prescribed by a doctor, different for each one—it depends on what their problem is. Mostly the pills calm them down so they can concentrate."

"They sure don't act very calm," said a boy.

"How can they?" smiled Miss Fish. "Up came the pills, along with everything else!"

She saw a few grins.

"Why did they have to be selfish and pig the bow?" asked a girl. "That's the best place to see from."

"Not selfish, my dear. Believe it or not, they were afraid. They were afraid if they gave up their places for even a minute, they'd never get them back. It's nothing new—they've been afraid all their lives. Afraid other boys and girls will laugh at them, or beat them in a game, or do better in their schoolwork. And that's usually the case. My children have been losers as long as they can remember. Can you imagine what it's like to be a loser most of the time? To drop the ball or come in last in a race or be clumsy and bump into things or have to take a grade over? My children have done all those things, and many more. So it really wasn't self-ishness—it was fear."

Dee-Dee flattened her nose against a cabin window. So did Mike.

There was a pause. It lasted and lasted. It became embarrassing. Miss Fish looked across the cabin at Mrs. Bellows, and the younger, bigger teacher dropped her eyes. Sarah Fish closed her own. Oh, please, please, one of you ask the big question, the only really important question, she implored silently. Isn't there one out of twenty who'll please, please ask it?

There was. It was Todd. "We're just beating around the bush," he said. "What's wrong with your kids?"

She opened her eyes. She could have adopted him. "They are neurologically impaired," she said quietly.

"Neuro-logic'ly impaired? What's that?"

She would have voted for Todd for President. "Their nervous systems don't work quite the way ours do," she explained. "It's because there was an accident when they were born, or because nature made some kind of mistake in their chemistry. Doctors aren't really sure. But the result is, their eyes and ears and arms and legs don't do what they should sometimes. Let me give you two examples—teachers are mad for examples, you know. One of my girls drops things or bumps into things or trips

89

or stumbles—and the reason is that even though her brain tells her arms and legs what they should do, they often won't, they won't obey her brain. And one of my boys painted a picture of our trip today to see the whales. But when he put the title at the top, he painted 'WHALES TO SEE THE.'"

Arnold's head appeared at a window.

"Whales to see the?" exclaimed a girl.

"That's right," said Miss Fish. "His brain won't let his eyes see things in proper order sometimes. Oh, there are all kinds of neurological impairments with big names —dyslexia, apraxia, hyperkinesia, dyscalculia, dysgraphia, auditory sequential memory, blah, blah, blah. But they all add up to the same thing—problems. And you'd be surprised how many children are born with such problems—more than seven million in the United States alone. Haven't you ever noticed in your own classes a few children who learn more slowly, who can't keep up with you—the losers—the boys and girls you laugh at and call 're-tards'?"

They had. They looked even sicker. And Miss Fish hurried on because she had no wish to make them so. "But they're not mentally retarded, they're just as intelligent and sensitive as you are. And underneath, they're just like you, too—they want to grow and learn and have fun and friends and achieve and be healthy and happy—but for them, it isn't easy. They have more burdens to bear than we do—burdens for which they are not to blame. So we have to help. We have to help them and respect them and try to understand their problems. We are all brothers and sisters to each other—did you ever think of that? Brothers and sisters to each other?"

She looked along the benches. Despite the gale outside, despite the pitching and rolling of *The Protector,* they were listening. Now's the time, she realized. So come on, Sarah girl, let's go.

Musette peeked into a window.

"I won't keep you much longer," said Sarah Fish. "But there's one last thing. You go on lots of trips with your teachers and parents, don't you? Well, my ten seldom do. Some of their parents haven't the money, others are afraid for their handicapped children, even ashamed of them in public. And so my ten have looked forward to today for a whole month—it was to be the grand and glorious adventure of the year for us." She paused. "But now, I understand from Mrs. Bellows, you want to go back to port. I don't blame you a bit. But if we turn tail, if we give up, my ten will lose again. We'll all lose. And I don't like to lose any more than you do. But why should we go on? You have a perfect right to ask. With weather like this, we can't see the whales anyway. Well, I'll tell you a secret."

Myron's head popped up at a window. Trying to see what was going on, he made funny faces.

"I have a hunch—a weenie, I call it—that if we stick it out—and we'll soon be at the Coronado Islands now—that if we do, a miracle may happen. Perhaps the weather will change. Perhaps we will see whales. I wouldn't bet on it, but I have a real weenie, with mustard and relish on it. So I'm going to ask you to vote. If most of you are willing to try, to go on, we will. But if most want to turn back, we'll do that. So what we do is entirely up to you."

Sarah Fish heaved a sigh. This is it, she thought. Now I'll know if I've accomplished something or if I've just been stacking BBs.

"All right," she said, "let me see the hands of those who want to go home."

Three hands were raised.

Whoopee, we've won! cheered Sarah Fish to herself.

"Now those who want to go on."

Two hands were raised.

Dammit, swore Sarah Fish silently.

"No," she said firmly, "that won't do. You must all vote. You must all look into your hearts and consciences and decide. I'll take another count. How many want to go home?"

This time nine hands went up.

"Nine. Now, how many are willing to take a chance on a miracle and go on?" She held her breath.

Eight hands were raised, then nine, ten, then eleven.

"Eleven!" she cried. "It's eleven to nine—we're going on!" She felt like dancing a jig. "Oh, thank you, my dears, thank you! I'm so grateful to—"

The scream which stopped her in mid-sentence was so shrill and bloodcurdling that it could be heard over the wind and waters and engines. It sliced through the walls of the cabin like a knife. It shot everyone inside 'to his feet, trying to see. But there were too many heads at the windows. They couldn't see who had screamed or why.

Her teacher knew one thing. Dee-Dee, only Dee-Dee,

was capable of such a scream.

There were only two cabin doors. Everyone inside attempted to get outside at once, scrambling and shoving, with the result that only two or three managed to get through each door in time to see.

Forward, near the bow, a boy stood for a terrible, endless instant on the rail.

Then he disappeared.

For the next minute, or two, or three—no one could later have told how long—there was complete chaos aboard *The Protector*.

Children burst in bunches from the cabin doors into the wind, over the rolling, pitching decks, falling down, crawling, lunging for the rails, pointing, babbling.

Miss Fish darted out, took one horrified look, let out a cry of anguish, and threw her arms about the bulk of Mrs. Bellows.

In the sea, on the white crest of a wave, the head of a boy appeared, a boy wearing glasses with hearing aids behind his ears.

On the bridge, Captain Murphy had seen it happen. He stopped the engines. He blew the boat's horn, a signal of disaster.

John's head went under water as the wave swept him away from the boat.

Captain Murphy tore open the wheelhouse door and yelled at Tony, who was standing aft, behind the cabin, combing his long hair, to throw a life preserver.

John's head emerged. He seemed to be making no effort to swim.

Near the cabin, another boy climbed onto the rail and dived overboard. It was Todd. He came up lashing at the water with powerful strokes.

Captain Murphy yelled a second time at Tony to throw a life preserver.

Tony threw his comb instead, realized what he had done, and froze.

Todd reached John. Their two heads foundered in foam and appeared again together.

Captain Murphy tore a life preserver from its rack on the bridge, crouched, cocked an arm, whirled, and threw.

The white ring sailed out over the sea, trailing its rope line, and splashed down close to the two boys. Todd seized it, and with one arm round John's neck, crooked his other arm through the ring.

Tony came to. Running forward, he took hold of the trailing line and began to haul it in, leaning back and bracing his shoes against the rail.

Several boys nearby began to help him, and presently many hands hauled at the line, pulling the two boys at the end of it closer and closer. Twice they were swamped by waves again, but each time the two heads bobbed up, faces streaming water.

Tony told his helpers to keep on hauling and everyone else to stand back. He removed the section of rail through which they had come aboard. Then, taking the line himself, he brought the preserver and boys alongside. He lay flat on the deck, holding himself with his left arm around a rail stanchion. Waiting till the boat rolled and dipped its deck almost level with the sea, he extended his right arm. Todd's hand reached for his, grasped it. And then, as the boat lifted again, rolling the other way, boys and life preserver were lifted as much by the power of the sea as by Tony, and with one last heave, Todd and John sprawled forward onto the deck, Todd's arm still choked about John's neck.

It was over.

Everyone was too exhausted to cheer, but several girls were crying.

A life had been saved, perhaps two.

The miracle that Captain Murphy had mentioned to his four young guests in the wheelhouse, that Sarah Fish had asked Mrs. Bellows' class to believe in, and to vote for, had taken place. But it was a different miracle.

Captain Murphy started the engines. *The Protector* made way again.

Everyone crowded around Todd and John, chattering at once. Someone asked John why he'd done it, but all he could do was splutter seawater. He couldn't hear the question anyway, for the batteries in his hearing aids were dampened and had gone dead.

Besides that, to his dismay Miss Fish gave him a kiss on top of his wet head. And Mrs. Bellows took Todd in a bear hug so grizzly that she almost crushed him.

The boys were soaked and shivering. Tony led them into the cabin, then belowdecks to a cubby locker where he kept spare clothing.

When they came up again, and out on deck, they wore

trousers six times too big, the legs rolled up above the ankles, and tied round the waist with rope, and John had on Tony's T-shirt with EAT YOUR HEARTS OUT, GIRLS! across the front.

Their wet clothes were slung up to Captain Murphy, who tied them to the mast to dry.

Boys and girls gathered round the heroes. John was asked again and again if he had meant to drown himself. Wanting to be friendly, he smiled and nodded yes each time, but it would have made no difference whether they had asked if the world was flat or the moon was made of green cheese—with his batteries dead, he was entirely out of touch. Todd, on the other hand, kept shaking his head and saying "No, he didn't mean to—I saw the whole thing. He was just trying to walk the rail without falling off. That takes a lot of cool, believe me. He just slipped, that's all." And he'd shake his head no and John would nod yes and everyone would make a face and stop trying to make sense of it.

When she had a chance, Dee-Dee took John by the wrist and dragged him aft, into a corner behind the cabin, and put her face close to his and spoke very slowly so that he could read her lips.

"Why did you do it?" she scolded.

"Because."

"Because is no answer. John, you tell me."

"Because I gave up. I do that a lot."

"But why?"

John the hero wrapped his oversized T-shirt around him tightly. "Well, I knew we wouldn't see any whales—

I told you last night we prob'ly wouldn't. That's the way it always is."

"It is not!" she snapped. "Anyway," she added, slowing down and forming each word perfectly, "you have no right to drown yourself now."

"Why not?"

"Because you have to be responsible now. Remember, you're almost a married man."

But something else had happened aboard *The Protector* besides a miracle, or a near-tragedy, or whatever it was. Boys and girls from both classes began to talk to each other. They talked about what they'd felt when they saw John in the water, and when Todd dived to his rescue. They laughed about Tony's throwing his comb instead of a life preserver. Children from Miss Fish's class found out from children in Mrs. Bellows' class what had transpired in the cabin during the meeting, about the vote to turn back or go on, and how close the outcome had been, eleven to nine. They talked about drugs and sports and school and records and teachers and movies and handicaps and parents. Names were exchanged. They forgot how sick they were, and how unlucky to have picked such a lousy day to see the whales, and how awful the weather was.

And they stood about the deck in twos and threes and fours and talked—boys with dyslexia and hyperkinesia and girls with freckles and bowlegs—boys with pimples and big ears and girls with dysgraphia and auditory sequential memory—tall and short and thin and fat and weak and strong and clumsy and athletic and handsome and homely and losers and winners—and forgot how seasick they were and how awful the weather was. They talked with such interest in each other that no one noticed he wasn't ill any more, wasn't blue or green or urpy, that in fact he felt as fit as a fiddle. They talked with such curiosity about each other that no one noticed the deck no longer rolled or pitched, that the waves had subsided, the wind had ceased to blow, the black clouds had pulled apart like a curtain before a stage, revealing a bright blue sky.

It was Miss Fish who made the discovery. "Why, those must be the Coronados!" she said. "Why, we're practically there!"

Several small, craggy islands loomed ahead off the starboard bow.

"Why, so we are!" exclaimed Mrs. Bellows.

Then one by one, the children began to crow like roosters in the dawning.

"Hey, the sun's out!"

"Hey, the storm's over!"

"Hey, I'm not seasick any more!"

"Hey, me neither! It's a nice day!"

When the horn on the funnel sounded a short blast, everyone jumped out of his skin and looked up at the bridge.

Captain Murphy stood in the sunshine, a grin on his face. "Good day. And now, young ladies and gents, allow me to introduce you to the gray whale."

"Where?" cried everyone. "Where?"

Captain Murphy spread his arms.

Two teachers and thirty youngsters rushed to the rails.

For a moment, they disbelieved. The surface of the ocean sparkled, blinding them. But from his higher perch, the captain could see what they could not—black shadows beneath the blue.

And then, not ten feet from the rail on the starboard side, a gray slab shoved the sea open. To those closest, it was bigger than a Greyhound bus, it was bigger than *The Protector* herself—nothing living on this earth could be that enormous! But it was, for next a head appeared, and a blowhole on top of the head opened, and, whufff! Then the head submerged, diving, and the back, and a tail lifted out of the water, the flukes waving as though to say good-by, and the whale sounded with such a thrust of the tail that those along the rail were showered!

For a moment, no one could utter a word. But when their hearts began to beat again, and they could breathe, one word was ripped from their throats:

"Wow!"

It was only the beginning. Another whale surfaced, this time on the port side, and another on the starboard, and another on the port, then groups of three, four, and five or more on both sides, forty or fifty in all. *The Protector* found herself in the center of a pod cruising north-ward, and Captain Murphy throttled the engines down so as to remain in the center, cruising with the pod at two to three knots. For the next half hour, those aboard the little boat watched from box seats a spectacle such as few humans are privileged to see.

The whales spouted.

They rose, opened their blowholes, and exhaled "Whufff!" The mist rising and making rainbows above their heads was not a spout of water from within them but the explosion of moisture collected on top of their blowholes while closed. Then they inhaled, filling their mighty lungs in a single breath, rolled, and dived, or sounded, to wave their tails good-by and swim submerged for several minutes before rising to spout again.

The whales spy-hopped.

Now and then one would stand upright, head and shoulders out of water, and seem to be getting his bearings or studying the strange breed of whale which had joined the pod, its orange-and-white back and sides as covered with calves as his own slate-gray back and sides were covered with scars and barnacles.

The whales breached.

Several of them leaped entirely free of the water as though to joy in their strength and freedom and dominion, their forty tons falling with a crash and splash which seemed to shake the ocean to its very bottom.

For the first few minutes of the spectacle, those privileged to witness it squealed and pointed and shouted and jumped up and down with delight. But after that, for twenty minutes perhaps, there was almost total silence aboard *The Protector*. No one moved about, no one sought a better place at the rails—at this feast for the senses there was enough for all. Boys and girls stood bewitched. It was a dream come true, a sight which no one there might ever behold again. And it was something more. For the first time the children thrilled to a kinship with creatures other than human. In their souls they began to understand that all living things, humble and magnificent, perfect and imperfect, are in fact one family, related and dependent, sharing one small planet, living one brief and precious life together. And so they stood bewitched, and watched the whales, and were one with each other as well.

It ended as abruptly as it had started. One minute the pod was rising and rolling and spouting and waving tails and sounding and spy-hopping and breaching and being as entertaining as it possibly could be at a children's matinee—and the next it was gone, into the deeps of the past, a memory the mind would cherish till death. The surface of the sea was untroubled. Sunlight danced upon it to no music except the monotone of the engines. A single seagull hung suspended from a sky as blue and kindly as an eye.

In the wheelhouse, Captain Murphy swung *The Protector* about and headed north-by-northeast, homeward bound. Twin throttles forward, the little vessel surged to fourteen knots, full speed, and took a bone in her teeth.

In the cabin, Miss Fish and Mrs. Bellows lunched together.

On the cabin roof, Tony the future movie star sat comfortably with his back to the funnel, tanning himself in the sun, admiring his muscles, and running fingers anxiously through his long black hair. He could scarcely wait to get back to port and lay his hands on a comb.

About the decks, fore and aft, the thirty youngsters sat in clusters eating lunch. All at once they were hungry as wolves. Mrs. Bellows' class shared its meal with Miss Fish's. John and Dee-Dee, Todd and Gloria sat together, Todd sharing with Dee-Dee, Gloria with John. "You really didn't try to drown yourself, did you, John?" she asked.

He nodded yes.

Todd shook his head no. "He was just trying to walk the rail without falling off. That takes cool, believe me. He just slipped."

"I wish you'd make up your minds," said Gloria.

Dee-Dee smiled at her. "John can't hear word one. His batteries are dead."

"Batteries?"

"In his hearing aids. From getting wet. What you have to do is speak slowly and form the words—then he can read your lips."

"Oh." Gloria leaned forward and spoke slowly, pronouncing each syllable of each word. "John, what kind of sandwich would you rather have? Chicken salad or peanut-butter-and-banana?"

John's mouth watered. He'd never tasted either. He felt sorry for the fishes feeding on his old baloney sandwich. "Both," he replied.

"Okay," said Gloria. "We'll each have a half of each."

"Todd, that was very brave of you to dive in after him," said Dee-Dee. She didn't mean to flatter him, but he really was groovy-looking.

"Not very," he said. "He wasn't far away, and it was good practice."

"Practice?"

"Sure. In a couple of years, when I'm fourteen, I'm going to try for a summer job as a lifeguard at Mission Beach. It pays real well, and mostly all you have to do is sit around and look at the chicks."

"A lifeguard, gee," said Dee-Dee, impressed. She was so impressed that she dropped part of her sandwich in her lap. "Nuts, I'm really clumsy today."

"Think nothing of it," he smiled. "We're just lucky we had today at all. When I think how close that vote was —yikes."

"What vote?" John asked with his mouth full. He couldn't decide which sandwich was the most heavenly, the chicken salad or the peanut-butter-and-banana.

"Our class, in the cabin," Gloria told him. "We voted to go back or keep going, and it was eleven to nine. Just one vote, a tie, and we'd have missed everything."

"Greatest sight I've ever seen, those whales," said Todd. "One of the best trips we've ever had. I'm sorry about the fight, though, and some rat in our class throwing your lunches overboard."

"Think nothing of it," Dee-Dee smiled.

"I was really mad," John said to Todd. "I'm just glad I didn't beat you to a pulp."

"Speaking of mad," said Dee-Dee, "I really am for Gary Garloo, aren't you, Gloria? I've got a big picture of him up in my room."

"Oh, he's okay."

"I think he's absolutely yummy," Dee-Dee enthused. "And I've bought every record he's made. Do you like him, Todd?"

"I don't listen to records much—I'm too busy after school playing ball. I like to pitch. Right now I'm working on my curve ball." Todd glanced at John and spoke slowly. "You play any sports, John?"

"He rolls tires," said Dee-Dee.

John gave her a dirty look.

"Rolls tires?" asked Todd.

Gloria changed the subject. "I have two kinds of cake, John—which would you like? Chocolate or coconut?"

John lip-read the question and hurriedly swallowed the last of the chicken salad and the peanut-butter-and-banana sandwiches and his mouth began to water again. Chocolate or coconut? He couldn't remember when he'd last had a piece of any kind of cake. In his opinion, Gloria wasn't good-looking, though she wasn't ugly either, but the more he ate, and the more she offered, the better-looking she became.

"Both," he said.

"I tell you, ladies, I've been bringing folks out here to see the whales for five years now, fall and spring, coming and going, and I've never stumbled onto a pod like that one before," Captain Murphy declared. "Nor have I ever seen 'em put on such a show. I tell you, ladies, you got your money's worth today."

He was standing at the wheel, Miss Fish at one side, Mrs. Bellows on the other. The three watched the two classes on deck below, sharing lunches and talking a mile a minute. Ahead of *The Protector,* off the port bow, was Point Loma, with its lighthouse, while off the starboard bow, rose-colored in the late afternoon sun, lovely and familiar, the city of San Diego glittered.

"And all thanks to you, Sarah," said Mrs. Bellows. "In my estimation, this has been the finest learning experience my class has ever had—and I don't mean just the whales, either. You know what I mean. And when I think we might have turned back, might have missed it, but for you!"

Miss Fish was embarrassed. "Don't thank me, please, Bertha." She tossed her head. "Which reminds me, I must stop at school on the way home and get a new set of batteries for John's hearing aids—we keep a spare set there."

She looked straight ahead, but land and sea were blurred by a tear in her eye. Dammit, don't be an old softie, Sarah girl, she ordered herself. Be a prim and proper spinster and blow your nose.

She blew her nose. "In any case, it truly was a grand and glorious adventure," she said. And then, to keep from getting teary again, she thought she'd have a bit of fun with the captain. "Ah, Captain," she began, "Have you ever seen a nicer day in these waters?"

He sensed what was coming. He set his jaw. "Well now, ma'am, it is pretty nice, I'll have to admit."

"And have you ever, in all your years, seen such a sudden, miraculous change in the weather?"

She was cornering him. He ran a finger round the collar of his shirt. "Well now, ma'am, it's pretty fickle out here sometimes."

"Fickle?" pried Miss Fish.

"I will admit, though," he said, surrendering, "that the wind died like somebody snuffed it out."

Sarah Fish smiled a spry-hearted, I-swallowed-a-goldfish smile. "I told you, Captain. Leave it to the Lord."

Captain Murphy adjusted his cap, took steady hold of the wheel with both hands, and looked exactly as the master of a seagoing vessel should look.

"No thank you, ma'am," he said. "I'll leave it to the Weather Bureau."

But the day was not yet ended. Miss Fish had another moment with her ten.

When they were on land again and reached the Volkswagen bus and clambered in, she closed the door and slid behind the driver's wheel—but instead of starting the motor and backing up and pulling out and gunning lickety-split onto the freeway and standing their hair on end while she tore past trucks and cement mixers and police cars, she just sat there. They waited.

"I forgot," she said. "But we don't need our second pills today, do we?"

"No," they said.

They thought she would start the bus then, but she didn't, she just sat there. They waited. They looked at her, wondering. She looked into the rear-view mirror and met the ten pairs of eyes.

"Now," she said softly, "one last thing. Let's pretend."

"Pretend what?" they asked.

"For a minute, let's pretend we're not here, that we're in our room at school, in an office. All of us together, in an office. Then close your eyes and listen with me."

"Listen?" they asked. "To what?"

"You know," she said.

Then she waited. Finally they caught on and said "Oh" and closed their eyes and she closed hers, and together, sitting quietly in the bus on the waterfront but pretending they were together in an office at school, shutting out the sounds of traffic and of ships, they listened in silence to the calling of the whales. To some, the sounds they made were like the bellowing of mighty ships in harbor. To others, the sounds were those of great gold and silver horns blown long and loud and echoing from mountain peak to mountain peak. Some thought the sounds were sad, others thought they were full of joy and life unbounded. To everyone, however, they were new and rare and beautiful.

Teacher and class opened their eyes. Hers met theirs in the rear-view mirror—Sandra's and Arnold's and Musette's and Myron's and Dee-Dee's and Pablito's and Mike's and Ralph's and Anne's and John's—and theirs were wide with wonder at the songs from under the sea, songs without words, songs as old as the oceans and as new as hope.

Anne spoke for them all. "Oh, Miss Fish," she whispered.

"Yes," said Sarah Fish. "Yes."

four

Dee-Dee's telephone rang that night as she lay in her room gazing at the poster picture of Gary Garloo on the wall but dreaming about Todd. She picked up the phone on the tabletop beside her bed. When a voice said "Dee-Dee, this is Todd. Remember me?" she nearly dropped it.

"Hello?" she gulped. "Hello? Hello?"

"Dee-Dee?"

"Who is this?"

"Todd. Remember me, on the boat today?"

No one had ever called her, especially no boy. She thought she might faint. "Todd? Let me think." She pretended to be thinking. "Oh yes, Todd. How are you?"

"Fine. And you?"

"Fine." Dee-Dee sat up in bed and tried to get out and tangled her legs in the sheets.

"Great day, wasn't it?" he asked.

She could have torn the sheets in two with her bare hands if she hadn't had to hold onto the phone with both hands for fear she'd drop it. "Yes, it was," she said. "Lis-

ten, Todd, I want to thank you for saving John's life."

"A mere bagatelle," he said.

"Bagatelle?" It was a new word to Dee-Dee, and it made her as furious as the sheets.

"Nothing," said Todd. "A bagatelle's something that's nothing."

"Oh." Finally she got her legs untangled and sat on the side of the bed in a most poised and adult position. "Well, thank you anyway. I know he wasn't playing any game—he actually tried to drown himself. John gets very depressed sometimes." She emphasized the word "depressed." "He's very sweet, but very—immature."

"Oh."

"And say, can you ever swim, Todd," she went on. "That's my favorite sport, too. I'm a terrific swimmer."

"Really?"

"You better believe it. Incidentally, you said when you're fourteen you're going to try to get a summer job as a lifeguard. How much does a lifeguard make?"

"Yikes, I don't know."

"Enough to get married?"

"Married? Married! How should I know? I mean, I don't know. Why?"

"Oh, I just wondered."

He wasn't pretending. She could almost hear him thinking.

"Well, listen, Dee-Dee, why I called," he said. "I was talking to your teacher, Miss Fish, just before we got off the boat, and she said you'd be coming to regular school this fall—the same junior high I'm going to."

"That's right. The same one?" She felt fainty again.

"But I didn't know it'd be your school."

"Well, it will. Anyway, what I wanted to say was, you'll be welcome, and you'll have a friend. We'll see a lot of each other, Dee-Dee, and I'll help you any way I can. You know, like carry your books and stuff."

"Oh," she said. She considered. It was too dreamy to be true. So she became suspicious. "How come?" she asked.

Todd hesitated. "Because I think you're Miss Wonderful," he said, then said quickly, "goodnight, Dee-Dee."

She tried to say goodnight but simply couldn't get the word out in time, for when she did, he was gone. She collapsed on the bed. Then she bounced up against her pillow. "Oh, wow!" she whispered to herself. "I might go out of my mind!"

No, she thought, I'll do no such thing. That's what a child would do, and I'm twelve going on thirteen, also apraxic and hyperkinetic, so I'm definitely not a child. What I'll do is, I'll call John.

She looked in the book found his number, and dialed, but the line was busy.

She waited a minute and dialed again. It was still busy. His mother must be a non-stop talker, and a windbag besides, she thought. Because it couldn't be John on the phone. He had nobody to call. And who'd call him but her?

When his bratty brothers and sisters came running into his room yelling "Telephone! Telephone! It's a girl! It's a girl!" John was sure it was Dee-Dee again, wanting to get married. He thought it might be a good idea to have his mother answer and say that he, John, had been taken to the hospital to have his tonsils and adenoids and appendix and a couple of other things cut out or that he had just enlisted in the Marines and been shipped to Iceland or the Sahara Desert for two or three years. But he put on his shoes and glasses and hearing aids and went out into the living room. They'd been watching roller derby all evening, but now the TV was off and the five of them, even his mother, were standing around with their ears wiggling, just waiting to find out who it was and what he would say. He foxed them again by placing the phone on the windowsill, closing the window on the cord, then going outside the house and picking up the phone. His brothers and sisters peered into the darkness and made dumb faces, but he knew they couldn't hear.

"Hello?" he said.

"John?"

"Yes."

"Hello, John. This is Gloria."

"Who?"

"Gloria. Don't you remember me, on the boat today?"

"Oh, sure. Hi." His mouth began to water at once at the memory of her chicken salad and peanut-butter-and-banana sandwiches. "How are you?"

"Fine," she said. "How are you?"

"Fine. Hey, thanks for sharing your lunch with me today."

"You're welcome," she said. "Wasn't it a good trip,

though? Weren't those whales something else?"

"Was it ever. Were they ever."

There was a pause.

"How come you called me?" he asked.

"Well," said Gloria, "just before we got off the boat today I was talking to your teacher, Miss Fish, and she said you'd be coming to regular school this fall—the same junior high I'm going to."

"No kidding. The same one?"

"That's right. And I just wanted you to know I'll be your friend, John. Maybe I'll come home with you after school someday, and you can show me how to roll tires. It sounds like fun."

"It is," he assured her. "It's really neat."

"Anyway, we'll see a lot of each other and I'll help you all I can. You know, like helping you remember to take your pills and things like that."

"Oh. Well, thanks." John almost added okay, anything you want as long as you lug along plenty of that chocolate and coconut cake to school every day. But then he thought of something else. Gloria was a girl, and being friendly, so there must be a catch somewhere. "You sure you're not just feeling sorry for me because I tried to drown myself?"

There was another pause.

"No, I'm not," said Gloria. And then she said, quickly, "I just think you're really far out, John. Goodnight," and hung up before he could reply.

Gollee, thought John, putting the phone back on the windowsill. Dee-Dee last night, Gloria tonight. I may be small and a little deaf and sometimes I don't see straight, but I'm really getting popular.

Suddenly the phone rang.

He let it ring three times before picking it up because he was certain it must be a wrong number.

"Hello?" he said.

"Hello. John?"

"Yes. Who's this?"

"Dee-Dee."

"Oh."

"How are you?"

"Fine."

"Do your hearing aids work okay? Did you get new batteries?"

"Yup."

"Say, your mother must be a really big talker," said Dee-Dee. "I dialed and dialed, but every time the line was busy."

"That was me," said John.

"You? Calling who?"

"Nobody. She called me."

"She? Who?"

"Gloria."

"Gloria!"

"Maybe you don't remember her. She was on the boat today. She was the one with the chicken salad and—"

"All that food—I remember her. If she doesn't watch it, she's going to be fat as a pig. Whatever did she want?"

"Well, she said she might come home after school

with me someday this fall and I could show her how to roll tires."

"She didn't."

"Yes, she did."

There was a pause.

"That was nice of her," said Dee-Dee.

"Wasn't it."

There was another pause.

"Todd called me."

"That was nice of him," said John.

"Wasn't it."

There was another pause.

"How come you called me?" John asked.

"Well, I've been thinking," said Dee-Dee. "John, I don't think we should get married right away after all."

"No kidding."

"No," she said. "After all, we're both going to regular school next fall, to junior high, and there'll be scads of kids. So I think we both ought to be free to look around —you know, to play the field."

"You're prob'ly right," said John.

"I hope this won't depress you too much, John," she said warmly.

"I'll be okay. I'll live."

"Promise me you won't try to drown yourself again or anything stupo like that?"

"I won't. Promise me you won't try to burn down your house or anything dumb like that?"

"I won't."

There was another pause.

"We'll always be friends, won't we, John?"

"Sure. Why not?"

"That's good." Dee-Dee seemed relieved. "Well, it's been nice talking to you. See you tomorrow. Goodnight, John."

"Goodnight, Dee-Dee."

John placed the phone on the windowsill and waited. If it had rung again, and been for him again, and been some girl again, he wouldn't have been in the least surprised. Up to last night, he thought, nobody ever telephoned me in my life. Now I've had three calls in two nights and all from girls. I bet that's going to be my biggest problem from now on—not dyslexia or impaired hearing or my mother or her "boyfriend" bottles or my brothers or sisters but girls. I must be a lot better-looking than I thought. Why, if I grew a mustache or a beard I'd prob'ly never get off the phone. Or there must be a bunch of other things about me they just can't resist. But I'm not getting hooked or going steady or getting married for a long, long time. Play it cool in regular school—that's my motto. So EAT YOUR HEARTS OUT, GIRLS!

Todd was reaching for the phone to call Gloria when it rang. "Todd?"

"Hi, Gloria. I was about to call you."

"Well, I beat you. Well, did you call her?"

"Sure did."

"What'd you say?"

"Just what we planned. That I was talking to her teacher, old Fish, just before we got off the boat, and found out she was coming to our school this fall and I just wanted her to know she'd have a friend et cetera et cetera. You know, the routine."

"What'd she say?" Gloria asked.

"I think she about had a heart attack."

"No wonder. I bet that's the first phone call she's ever had from a boy."

"Probably." Todd yawned. "You called what's-his-name?"

"John. Yes. I told him the same thing, practically word for word, Miss Fish and all."

"Did he believe it?"

"All the way. You know what I even offered to do?"

"What?"

"Go home with him someday after school and have him show me how to roll tires." Gloria giggled. "Can you imagine? Roll tires?"

"You really went all-out."

"I really did. Now I suppose he thinks he's Gary Garloo or somebody. Incident'ly, I can't stand Gary Garloo, can you?"

"No."

They were silent. They were thinking the same thing, but each wanted the other to say it first.

Todd said it. "Well, I guess we've done our good deed for the day."

"I hope so. I hope Bellows is satisfied—it was her idea we call them and be buddies, not mine."

"Mine either."

"And I'm not being mean," Gloria added. "I will be nice to John, but nice and nothing else. I'm not tying myself down next year to any boy who wears hearing aids and tries to commit suicide."

"You're smart," Todd said. "I'm not getting thrown for a loss by that Dee-Dee, either. Sure, I'll be polite and say hello and stuff, but any girl who stumbles and bumbles around is off my list. I'm going to be an athlete. I'm interested in co-ordination."

"I don't blame you," Gloria agreed. "You're too normal—we both are. Anyway, I think people should solve their own problems, and not be so dependent on others."

"So do I." Todd yawned. "Listen, Gloria, thanks for calling, but I've got to sack out. I'm sort of in training."

"Okay. Goodnight, Todd, see you tomorrow." She giggled again. "Roll tires!"

"Goodnight." He laughed. "Gary Garloo!"

Under the reaches of the sea the pod moved northward in the night. It moved in straight lines, and slowly, for the journey it must make was long beyond belief. It needed no star to steer by. No storm or tide could turn it from its course. It was composed of living things which understood one another, of creatures which would guide and protect and care for one another until together, together, all had climbed the ocean to their journey's end.

ABOUT THE AUTHORS

KATHRYN and GLENDON SWARTHOUT, have written a candid and realistic story about the difficulties children with learning disabilities face everyday, not only from their impairments but, also, from the attitudes of their families and of society. Both began as teachers, he of university literature courses and she in elementary school. They have written four other novels for children, and Mr. Swarthout has also written many novels for adults including, WHERE THE BOYS ARE and BLESS THE BEASTS AND CHILDREN. Mr. and Mrs. Swarthout live in Scottsdale, Arizona.

PAUL BACON was born in Ossining, New York. He became a jazz critic and graphic artist and studied briefly in S. W. Hayter's Atelier 17. He discovered an interest in publishing and formed his own studio in the 1950s. Mr. Bacon, his wife, seventeen-year-old son and two cats and an otter hound live near New Paltz, New York.